The Effective Teaching of Mathematics

THE EFFECTIVE TEACHER SERIES

General editor: Elizabeth Perrott

The Effective Teaching of Mathematics

Malcolm Simmons

Longman
London and New York

Longman Group UK Limited
Longman House, Burnt Mill,
Harlow Essex CM20 2JE, England
and Associated Companies throughout the world.

*Published in the United States of America
by Longman Publishing, New York*

© Longman Group UK Limited 1993

First published 1993
ISBN 0-582-01633-9

British Library Cataloguing-in-Publication Data

A catalogue record for this book is
available from the British Library

Library of Congress Cataloging-in-Publication Data

Simmons, Malcolm, 1944-
The effective teaching of mathematics / Malcolm Simmons
    p. cm. -- (The Effective teacher series)
    Includes bibliographical references and index.
    1. Mathematics--Study and teaching. I. Title. II. Series.
QA11.S565 1993
510'.712--dc20   91-47727
                                                            CIP

Set by 7E in 10pt Times

Printed in Hong Kong
WC/01

To my parents
Eric and Irene Simmons

CONTENTS

EDITOR'S PREFACE

This new series was inspired by my book on the practice of teaching (*Effective Teaching: a Practical Guide to Improving your Teaching*, Longman, 1982), written for trainee teachers wishing to improve their teaching skills as well as for in-service teachers, especially those engaged in the supervision of trainees. The books in this series have been written with the same readership in mind. However, busy classroom teachers will find that these books also serve their needs as changes in the nature and pattern of education make the in-service training of experienced teachers more essential than in the past.

The rationale behind the series is that professional courses for teachers require the coverage of a wide variety of subjects in a relatively short time. So the aim of the series is the production of 'easy to read', practical guides to provide the necessary subject background, supported by references to guide and encourage further reading, together with questions and/or exercises devised to assist application and evaluation.

As specialists in their selected fields, the authors have been chosen for their ability to relate their subjects to the needs of teachers and to stimulate discussion of contemporary issues in education.

The series aims to cover subjects ranging from the theory of education to the teaching of mathematics and from primary school teaching and educational psychology to effective teaching with information technology. It will look at aspects of education as diverse as education and cultural diversity and pupil welfare and counselling. Although some subjects such as the legal context of teaching and the teaching of history are specific to England and Wales, the majority of the subjects such as assessment in education, the effective teaching of statistics and comparative education are international in scope.

Elizabeth Perrott

AUTHOR'S PREFACE

This book is for all those concerned with the mathematical education of children in secondary schools, but in particular for those in the process of becoming mathematics teachers, for those experienced teachers contemplating a change to mathematics teaching and for those mathematicians who are in the early stages of their mathematics teaching careers.

The book provides an overview of mathematics teaching at secondary level and links established mathematics content to recent curriculum developments in mathematics teaching in England and Wales and in Scotland.

The main purpose of the book is to instigate and complement good mathematics teaching practice in our classrooms. To this end the presentation is such that readers are led across and into a number of different activities designed

> to build confidence
> to improve awareness of teaching situations and strategies
> to improve awareness of the processes involved in learning and doing mathematics
> to help gain experience of available resources.

There is a gradual increase in complexity, concentrating initially on skills required in making a good start. Different approaches to the teaching of mathematics are considered, linking general skills of questioning and discussion with specific topics. Ways of enriching the mathematical experience of all pupils through discussion, problem solving and mathematical investigation form an important part of the book. A whole chapter is devoted to problem solving and mathematical investigation. This reflects the importance given to these aspects of mathematics education in recent years and the author's view that the process of teacher as problem solver is an important factor in pupils becoming good problem solvers. There is a final chapter on the use of Logo as an aid to creating new and exciting mathematical environments which pupils and teachers can explore together. A number of earlier themes are returned to in the context of Logo programming, and a list of procedures used in this chapter, written in Logotron Logo, is given in an appendix. Many diagrams accompany the text throughout the book, reflecting the author's belief in the power of diagrams for augmenting and developing mathematical thinking.

Throughout the book there are extensive references to relevant research findings. It is hoped that such references will introduce readers to the important role of research in mathematics education which may subsequently move them towards a more research-based approach when reflecting on the possible need for changes in current practice.

Malcolm Simmons
University of Stirling

ACKNOWLEDGEMENTS

We are grateful to the following for permission to reproduce copyright material;

Heinemann Educational Books, Inc for a list of headings from *From Communication to Curriculum* by Douglas Barnes (1976, 1992); the Controller of Her Majesty's Stationery Office for an extract from *Curriculum Matters 3, Mathematics from 5–16* (HMSO, 1985), extracts from *Mathematics in the National Curriculum* (HMSO, 1989), extracts from *Mathematics for Ages 5 to 16* (DES, 1988) & an extract from *Microcomputers and Mathematics in Schools* by T J Fletcher (DES, 1983); Simon & Schuster Education, Hemel Hempstead, for extracts from *Thinking Things Through* by L Burton; ILECC and the Smile Centre for Newtiles program in the microSMILE series; Springer-Verlag Gmbh & Co KG and the author D W Crowe for our Figure 2.11, adapted from Figure 6 in *The Geometric Vein* (1981); B T Batsford Ltd for our Figure 2.15, reproduced page 100 from *Abstract Design* (1930) by A Fenn; Cambridge University Press for our Figure 2.16 being the last pattern of Figure 13 on page 125 from *Topics in Recreational Mathematics* (1970) by J H Cadwell; NFER-Nelson for our Figures 2.18–2.21 from *Fractions: Children's Strategies and Errors* (1986) by D Kerslake and our Figures 2.23 and 2.24 from *Children's Mathematical Frameworks 8–13* (1989) by K Hart; Oxford University Press for our Figure 3.5, adapted from Figure 19 in *The Mathematics of Great Amateurs* (1990) by J L Coolidge; D O K Publishers, Buffalo, NY, 14224 for our Figure 4.1 from *Classroom Ideas for Encouraging Thinking and Feeling* Vol I (1970), by Frank Williams; The Mathematical Association for our Figure 4.14 adapted from a figure in *Mathematics in School* Vol 18 No 4, September 1989.

We have been unable to trace the copyright holder in the following and would appreciate any information that would enable us to do so:

the figure 'Towers of Hanoi' adapted from McGregor and Watt *Advanced Programming for the BBC Micro* (1983).

CHAPTER 1

Approaches to teaching and learning mathematics

During the last decade two reports have provided significant guidelines for practising mathematics teachers and for those training to become mathematics teachers to help bring about more effective teaching in their classrooms. These are *Mathematics Counts: Report of the Committee of Inquiry into the Teaching of Mathematics in Schools* (the Cockcroft Report: DES 1982) and *Mathematics from 5 to 16: Curriculum Matters 3* (DES 1985). The former has had a significant impact on the deliberations for a national curriculum for mathematics in England and Wales, and has had some influence in the development of the mathematics curriculum in Scotland.

It is the purpose of this book not to judge to what extent these publications have been successful in bringing about change, but to attempt to offer the reader practical guidance towards becoming an effective mathematics teacher based upon the widely accepted principles set out in these publications. The book is aimed at those training to become mathematics teachers but it might also be of use to experienced teachers of other subjects wishing to teach mathematics.

Statutory orders detailing attainment targets and programmes of study now exist for the teaching of mathematics in England and Wales, and as yet non-statutory guidance of a similar nature exists in Scotland, but the inexperienced teacher is more likely to be concerned with the practicalities of 'having a good lesson' than with more distant but no less important questions concerning the teaching of mathematics in our schools. Because of these immediate considerations most relevance will be found in those parts of the reports dealing with 'approaches to' or 'styles of' teaching mathematics.

Mathematics from 5 to 16 states and discusses twelve principles influencing the approaches which might be adopted. These twelve principles enlarge upon the now famous paragraph 243 in the Cockcroft Report, which states the need for the following approaches to the teaching and learning of mathematics:

exposition by the teacher
discussion
appropriate practical work
consolidation and practice of fundamental skills

problem solving
investigative work.

It would be foolish and naïve to suggest that these principles generally or strictly adhered to would result in effective mathematics teaching, but they can be regarded as a good agenda for action. The quality of that action depends greatly upon the personal qualities of the teacher and the attitudes towards mathematics which can be engendered in pupils.

It is not suggested here, nor was it suggested in the Cockcroft Report, that mathematics teaching in any one lesson should fall only into one or two of these categories. However, it will be useful to consider briefly each one separately in order to appreciate the quite different demands each has on the teacher and pupils.

Exposition

Exposition is probably the aspect of teaching which the trainee teacher readily relates to as the 'teaching act', and in which he/she feels the most measureable gains are to be made as training proceeds; indeed, it is an aspect upon which many judgements are to fall. It is quite likely that this was the style followed by the student's own teachers for much of the time and so is well within his/her experience.

This approach to classroom teaching, particularly if the whole class is being addressed, puts the teacher in the spotlight, usually centre stage, and the demands are not dissimilar to those of an actor with an expectant audience. Effectiveness in this situation requires many skills and attributes. The most important ones for the trainee teacher to concentrate on initially are:

to have, or at least show, confidence in the material being presented
to communicate in a clear, unhurried, unambiguous manner.

If these do not come easily to the student then extra effort and guidance will be needed. Without these two basic requirements exposition will be ineffective or, worse, harmful to the progress of pupils. It is here that the similarity with the actor's role ends; the pupil audience should take an active role in the proceedings, not a passive one.

Together with the need to present situations efficiently and to hold centre stage whilst doing so, the teacher also needs to stimulate pupils into thinking about and contributing to the topic under discussion. This requires skills which are more difficult to acquire, and during initial attempts the student will feel less secure, less sure of where things are going, less centre stage and more anxious about fulfilling objectives.

More will be said of this later. Done well, exposition can be a rich and rewarding classroom approach.

Successful exposition may take many different forms but the following are some of the qualities which should be present: it challenges and provokes the pupils to think; it is reactive to pupils' needs and so it exploits questioning techniques and discussion; it is used at different points in the process of learning and so, for example, it may take the form of pulling together a variety of activities in which the pupils have been engaged; and it uses a variety of stimuli. (DES 1985 : 38)

Discussion

It may appear from the previous quotation that bringing about discussion in the mathematics classroom is but a simple step away from a lesson in which the teacher has successfully achieved his objectives through exposition. The role which pupils will take relies heaviiy on the implications behind the word 'exploits'. How does the teacher exploit questioning techniques and discussion? How is discussion generated? What demands are made on pupils? What skills are needed by the teacher?

These and other questions will be dealt with in greater detail in Chapter 5. The aim here is to give the reader some feeling for what lies behind the concept of good discussion in a mathematics classroom. Good discussion will not just happen, it has to be planned for, worked at and practised. It essentially requires a shift in the established roles of many teachers and their pupils. If the trainee teacher can begin to develop this as a possible classroom approach along with other approaches right from the start of training, much will be gained by not having to make such a deliberate change in approach later on, and a much more flexible attitude towards teaching and learning will be developed. Pupils too will gradually adapt and become more active and more responsible for their own learning. Clearly in order to have good discussion there must be something worthy of discussion, and the organizational factors for facilitating that discussion need some careful thought. Planning will inevitably be less detailed about where the lesson is to go, but this does not mean that there should be less planning; on the contrary, it is very likely that this approach will demand a far wider preparation than hitherto experienced.

One of the most inhibiting factors against the development of discussion in the secondary classroom has been the presence of public examinations and to a lesser extent the internal examination. As examination time looms nearer, lessons become more dedicated to the preparing of pupils for the type of examination questions they are likely to get, rather than taking a more extensive format in which pupils are active, develop ideas by doing, refine ideas by discussing and even arguing, and reflect on findings. The new examination syllabuses and curricular guidelines now give encouragement to follow a wider approach. The following two assessment objectives are included in the National Criteria for mathematics:

Any scheme of assessment will test the ability of candidates to:
3.16 respond orally to questions about mathematics, discuss mathematical ideas and carry out mental calculations;
3.17 carry out practical and investigational work, and undertake extended pieces of work. (SEC 1986)

In describing how 'contexts for learning', 'kinds of learning' and 'aspects of mathematics' interrelate, the Report of the Review and Development Group on Mathematics for Scotland, *Mathematics 5–14* (SED 1990) stresses the importance of identifying a context, developing positive attitudes and awareness, and using problem solving to learn concepts, facts and skills. Appropriate discussion between teacher and pupils and amongst pupils themselves can play a major part in bringing about these desirable outcomes.

Appropriate practical work

It is unfortunate that much practical work in mathematics is confined to the least able groups. This practice reinforces attitudes that mathematics, 'respectable mathematics', is highly abstract and that resorting to simple models and apparatus detracts from the true spirit of mathematics. It is through appropriate practical work, the emphasis being on the word 'appropriate', that ideas about what doing mathematics really is can begin to change. The sensitive use of practical work can be a great unifying factor within a classroom, providing a means to seek common goals, to share ideas and experiences and to delight in corporate success.

Practical work in the mathematics classroom need not always be directly related to the needs of employers or to the direct or more obvious needs of individuals seeking employment. There will always be a place for such approaches but not to the exclusion of the experiential, often very simple approaches designed to develop mathematical thinking within the individual which leads to a clearer understanding of the concepts involved. It is through the use of such practical work that the inexperienced teacher is likely to become more aware of the importance of the processes experienced by the pupils, and to realize that mathematics teaching is not concerned merely with the identification and acquisition of techniques to be remembered and demonstrated at a predetermined future date.

Appropriate practical work also provides the teacher with an excellent opportunity to learn more about the children, to learn names and faces, to find out what level of thinking each child is capable of, to diagnose weaknesses without testing and to provide help without taking away initiative. It provides space and time to think!

Consolidation and practice of fundamental skills

The student teacher is likely to find considerable pressure brought to bear on this aspect of teaching – a pressure which has for many years dominated all too easily the pattern of lessons. This is highlighted by the often heard criticisms of new mathematics schemes that allegedly do not provide sufficient practice of fundamental skills. Trainee teachers will of course need to discover the importance of such skills and where necessary diagnose weaknesses and teach explicitly towards them. The teacher should however be developing ideas about creating situations where the need to have certain skills becomes apparent to the learner. Motivating pupils in this way is extremely important if the teacher is to avoid the drudgery of mere practice lessons. This naturally leads into the introduction of problem solving.

Problem solving and investigative work

Mathematical problem solving should be an accepted integral part of any mathematics programme. By 'accepted' I mean accepted on the part of the pupils. On the one hand it should not be regarded by them or the teacher as an add-on activity requiring little attention, and on the other hand pupils should not become over-anxious and worried at the prospect of not being able to cope with a problem situation. Given sufficient planning and preparation, this aspect of mathematics learning can be the most rewarding and enjoyable for all concerned.

Situations where pupils can be motivated – and motivated for the right reasons (i.e. task motivated) – should never be far from view when lessons are planned or evaluated. In fact motivation could always be included in a lesson plan as an unwritten but assumed aim of any lesson. Matching problems to pupil abilities and past experiences is a major factor affecting motivation. If we assume for the moment that a good match can be made and that other factors are present which produce the kind of classroom where thinking can take place, then motivation for many will be directed into action, and largely negative non-cognitive affects such as anxiety, pressure and non-perseverance which naturally arise during the problem-solving process will have less impact.

Interest in problem solving has widened from eminent researchers such as Polya (1945) and Wickelgren (1974), who advocated that the right kind of experiences could improve problem-solving skills, to educationalists and teachers who are now faced with developing these activities in the classroom. The nature of problem solving in the classroom is continuing to change as teachers and pupils become more familiar with modern technology. A growing familiarity is a prerequisite for skilful use, but it is unlikely to be sufficient for those who take on a personal responsibility for course development and effective assessment. An awareness of possibilities and the courage to take risks in both planning and execution of lessons are also very necessary. This I know asks a lot of inexperienced teachers who naturally will tend to take a safer line, but exposure for them to the possible uses of modern technology in developing courses is going to be greater than ever before.

There should be no tasks for which pupils are *required* not to use new technology, unless a very strong case can be made. The number of such cases is likely to be very small. (Report of Joint Mathematical Council Conference on National Curriculum and Attainment Targets, 1987)

Chapters 3 and 7 consider these aspects in more detail. Orton (1987) comments upon a problem having a 'static feel about it' and an investigation as having an 'active feel about it', in the sense that the problem definition does not change substantially as the process to a solution continues, whereas the investigation process is more open ended and problem posing becomes an equal partner with problem solving in the total process of investigative mathematics. To my mind it is the problem posing aspect of an investigation which sets it apart from other activities. However, good use of the modern microcomputer and appropriate software makes the distinction between investigations and problem solving operationally unimportant as one becomes part of the other more readily than ever before. The potential uses of existing and more sophisticated technologies such as interactive video have many implications for the ways in which we conduct classroom experiences. There are also many considerations to be made by trainers and trainees alike during a course of teacher training regarding how best to utilize information technology in teaching/learning situations.

This chapter has attempted by way of introduction to give a very brief overview of important aspects of mathematics teaching and learning. Each aspect will be returned to at different parts of this book but in differing teaching/learning situations. The next chapter considers in more detail some aspects of lesson preparation which the inexperienced teacher is likely to find useful.

Further reading

Ahmed A. 1987 *Better Mathematics: A Curriculum Development Study* HMSO

Buchanan N.K. 1987 Factors in problem solving performance *Educational Studies in Mathematics* 18(4): 399–415

Dessart D.J., Suydam M.N. 1983 Problem Solving. In Dessart D.J. (ed.) *Classroom Ideas from Research on Secondary School Mathematics* National Council of Teachers of Mathematics, Reston, Virginia, 29–38

Ernest P. (ed.) 1987 *Teaching and Learning Mathematics Parts 1 and 2* School of Education, University of Exeter, Part 1, 47–56

Orton A. 1987 *Learning Mathematics: Issues, Theory and Classroom Practice* Cassell, Chapter 6

CHAPTER 2

Some early considerations when planning lessons

If you are embarking upon a teacher training course it is likely that you will be asked to prepare part of a topic with a view to teaching that topic either to a small group of children or to a peer group of students. In either case a number of demands are immediately placed upon you as the teacher. The most likely are:

1. What topic, within mathematics, will you choose?
2. Which topics do you feel you know something about?
3. Which topics are you enthusiastic about and feel you can enthuse others?
4. What kinds of things do you want your pupils to learn?
5. What experiences do you want your pupils to have?
6. What do you know about your pupils and their abilities and experiences?
7. What ideas for presentation do you have?
8. Where can you find ideas?
9. What basic teaching skills will you try to use and develop?

Less urgent but equally important things to consider are:

1. How will you plan pupil experiences to facilitate learning?
2. What instructions or explanations do you envisage giving?
3. What questions will you ask?

Already these considerations seem too much to contemplate for a first attempt, and there may well arise a feeling of conflict between concentrating on your necessary development of skills and the needs of your pupils in a learning situation. If you are fortunate enough to practise these skills in a microteaching situation where small groups of children are involved for short periods, then concentrating on skills is going to be easier, but in any case the two requirements are not necessarily incompatible.

This particular period of training should be considered as the beginning of a process where you have the opportunity to concentrate on a number of basic teaching skills, to determine where your strengths and weaknesses as a communicator lie, to begin to gain knowledge of appropriate material within a small knowledge domain and to pursue a limited range of objectives with a small group. These objectives although limited in range should be concerned not merely with knowledge or content but with providing experiences which allow pupil learning to take place and which reveal learning needs. It is precisely this awareness of learning needs which triggers appropriate skilful action in the experienced teacher, and part of your responsibility in training and afterwards will be to develop this awareness, practise appropriate responses and evaluate their effectiveness.

The major distinctions between a microteaching situation and a whole class situation are summarised in Table 2.1.

Table 2.1 **Distinctions between microteaching and whole class teaching**

Microteaching	Whole class lessons
Small groups	Usually larger groups
Concentrating on particular teaching skills; limited organizational factors	Developing and combining teaching skills together with classroom management and organization
Limited short term objectives	Longer term objectives and goals as well as short term ones
Developing knowledge of curriculum material	Developing schemes of work in the school context; adjusting content and presentation to suit particular user groups
Learning how to be self-critical	Greater cognizance of pupil achievement; widening of the knowledge domain and interlinking with other concepts; developing powers of self-criticism

Content and pedagogy

It will be seen from Table 2.1 that microteaching as well as whole class lessons has a requirement for the teacher to be aware of the importance of and the need for a blend of good knowledge about the subject under discussion and the pedagogical knowledge of teaching. Much of what is presented in this book and how it is presented is influenced by the firm belief (supported by much research evidence) that in order to teach well the teacher needs to know about the subject matter in both width and depth to a degree unlikely to be found amongst those beginning (or indeed finishing) a teacher training course.

There has been much written about and much research into the general pedagogical principles considered as prerequisite to good teaching. The linking of these principles to a sound knowledge of the curriculum and the means by which this can be achieved have been less emphasized. Leinhardt and Smith (1985) define subject matter knowledge to include

concepts
algorithmic operations
connections amongst different algorithms
the subset of the number system being drawn upon
understanding of types of pupil errors
curriculum presentation

and they consider that various degrees of awareness of or facility with these aspects strongly influence how a lesson is planned for and taught. Shulman (1986) describes what he perceives as the lack of focus on the subject matter itself in teacher training courses, and how this is translated into action, or not as the case may be, as the 'missing paradigm'.

Similar feelings about the missing paradigm were succinctly expressed by a Yorkshire headteacher who, after watching students teach, described the lessons as having 'plenty of bridle and saddle but no hoss!' The 'hoss' refers to the body of the lesson, where the teacher not only uses pedagogical skills but brings to the situation his knowledge and experience of the subject matter. This is not brought about simply by looking to see what the next few pages of the recommended textbook have to offer. Subject knowledge for teaching has to take on a number of facets in order to be an effective source for innovation and inspiration. It is generally agreed that teacher trainers should avoid the giving of blueprints for particular (contrived?) situations. Instead they should develop courses where sound principles of good teaching are linked with the opportunity for the trainee to develop teaching skills together with 'knowledge for teaching' in order to respond in a positive and individual way to the particular circumstances prevailing at the time.

These different facets as described by Shulman are:

1. Content knowledge: the amount and organization of knowledge *per se*.
2. Pedagogical content knowledge: this goes beyond knowledge *per se* to knowledge for teaching, i.e. awareness of the relevant aspects of knowledge for teaching, and the teachability of what is known.
3. Curricular knowledge: knowledge of the curriculum and materials; 'tools of the trade' for presenting and exemplifying concepts and for evaluating pupils' progress.

Curricular knowledge means knowing about alternative texts; how simple materials can be used by teacher and pupils to demonstrate and elucidate their content; how software and programming skills can act as further sources of enrichment; what classes lower down and further up the school may be doing on related topics; and how you see what you are doing with your classes fitting into the larger scheme of work. There is also a requirement for a horizontal awareness of what other uses may be made of mathematics in other subjects and how other subject teachers perceive the role of mathematics in their subject.

Practicalities

So what topics, given the choice, are you going to consider? To help you decide where your initial strengths lie, Table 2.2 suggests books and periodicals which should help you to begin to develop a topic. The content of most of these is appropriate for the mainstream 11–13 age group, and most schemes mentioned go beyond this to senior secondary levels. You should make a point of reading some of the teachers' guides carefully; in this way you can profit from other teachers' experiences. There are few general guidelines that can be given in choosing a mathematical topic, but at this stage you should guard against thinking that teaching some aspect of number will be an easy option; it rarely is.

Table 2.2 **Sources for topic development**

School Mathematics Project (SMP), Booklets 1–4, Books G1, G2 (and Resource Pack A), B1, B2, Y1 and Y2. Check the ability range for which each has been designed
Journey into Mathematics South Notts Project; Teachers' Guides 1 and 2
Kent Mathematics Project (KMP) workcards; mainstream boxes 1, 2 and 3
Smile taskcards (ILEA). Also a list of commercial references linking to items on the Smile network. The network itself is a valuable source of references which cover similar themes
Mathematics in Action Books 1 and 2, Blackie-Chambers
Mathematics Teaching periodical, Association of Teachers of Mathematics
Mathematics in Schools periodical, Mathematical Association

What follows is intended to act as a guide in preparing yourself for teaching a topic. It takes the form of a discussion and information about a topic and some suggested teacher presentations and pupil experiences which you might find helpful in deciding which approaches to try. These are very much dependent upon the content and process objectives for the lesson. Objectives bring a lesson into focus and enable the planner to structure the lesson in a way which brings about desired learning. Achievement of objectives should also indicate in some way that learning has taken place.

Certain objectives of a general nature have now been formalized in the National Curriculum (NC) as attainment targets (ATs). These are defined as 'the knowledge, skills and understanding which pupils of different abilities and maturities are expected to have by the end of each key stage' (DES 1989). The end of each of the four key stages defined in the 1988 Education Reform Act roughly corresponds with the ages of 7, 11, 14 and 16. In the following discussion and throughout the book reference will be made where appropriate to attainment targets, their levels (1–10) and the corresponding programmes of study as given in the National Curriculum. Reference will also be made to the Report of the Review and Development Group on Mathematics for Scotland, *Mathematics 5–14* (SED 1990: abbreviated *5–14*). Tables 2.3 and 2.4 link the levels, age ranges and key stages in these two curricula. However, one of the aims of the book is that you should develop a feel for what is possible with pupils you come to know and not be constrained at a crucial stage of your own development by recent legislation.

Table 2.3 **National Curriculum levels and ages**

Level	Age	Key stage
1–3	4–7	1
2–6	8–11	2
3–8	12–14	3
4–10	14–16	4

Table 2.4 **Mathematics 5–14 levels and school years**

Level	School year
A	Primary 1 to primary 3
B	Primary 3 to primary 4
C	Primary 4 to primary 6
D	Primary 5 to primary 7
E	Primary 7 to secondary 2

Primary 7 in Scotland corresponds by age to secondary 1 (Year 7) in England and Wales.

You may find some of the following suggestions useful as they stand in preparation for your first attempt at teaching a small group, but do not be afraid to select your own objectives and to make your own interpretation of the subject matter and its presentation. What follows is to suggest a number of ways forward at this stage and is not given as a lesson plan exemplar to be used uncritically. It is not intended that you should attempt to achieve all that is presented here or to use all the suggested materials. Selection of materials with due consideration given to time limitations and the abilities of the group is a skill you will have to acquire early on if you are to present interesting and purposeful lessons. The amount of material prepared should always be sufficient for more than the planned time allowance, and eventually the type of material prepared should allow for the different abilities and perceptions that the group is bound to have.

The first topic chosen is symmetry, but preparation for other topics could follow similar lines.

Symmetry

Objectives

Learning about symmetry provides many opportunities of approach, and specific objectives can be listed which lie in each of the broader aims discussed in *Mathematics from 5 to 16* (DES 1985):

> facts
> skills
> conceptual structures
> general strategies
> personal qualities.

Recognizing symmetry in shapes and using simple transformations to generate symmetry patterns also feature widely in NC AT 11, shape and space, as follows:

> level 3 – reflective symmetry
> level 4 – rotational symmetry
> level 5 – identification of symmetries of various shapes
> level 6 – reflect simple shapes in a mirror line.

At all levels, learning about symmetry provides a good opportunity for building positive attitudes towards mathematics. However, although this is desirable, it does not help in any detailed planning of a teaching/learning situation; it simply gives us (teachers not pupils) one good reason for including it in a scheme of work or syllabus. To develop greater spatial awareness in our pupils and more specifically to generate interest in symmetrical shapes are both praiseworthy goals which teachers should be aware of, but neither is of much help in the planning of a particular lesson.

For objectives to bring focus to a lesson they have to be short term and explicit. However, focus must not be interpreted to mean a narrowing of ideas and approaches. There may well be a number of desired outcomes to a lesson and a number of teaching strategies employed (the Cockcroft Report paragraph 243 again: see Chapter 1), and it is largely the nature of the stated objectives which will determine the approaches adopted.

What learning outcomes can one reasonably expect from introductory sessions on symmetry? Answers to questions like this are more likely to produce usable objectives.

Some specific objectives might be as follows:

1. To generate activities where pupils decide on simple rules for producing symmetrical patterns (NC AT11 level 2; *5–14* level B).
2. Pupils to cut out a number of specified paper shapes, to find the number of ways of 'posting' these through the hole that is left and to form a table to enable them to distinguish between rotational and bilateral symmetry (NC AT11 levels 4 and 5).
3. To encourage pupils to produce their own shapes exhibiting each kind of symmetry (NC AT11 levels 4 and 5; *5–14* level D).
4. To encourage pupils to describe the shapes they have produced (transcends all levels).
5. To be able to analyse simple patterns for symmetry (NC AT11 level 6; *5–14* level E).

Notice that some objectives are concerned with the actual topic whilst others relate to the classroom processes through which learning is to take place.

The reader might like to undertake the following exercise:

1. Try to determine where each of the above objectives lies in relation to knowledge, skills, understanding and use of shape and space as set out in the National Curriculum.
2. Try to write your own specific objectives which keep a balance between these four areas.
3. For each objective try to determine the nature of the learning envisaged. For example, will the learning be directed with little room for deviation? Will it be more open and allow for more divergent thinking or creativity? Will pupils benefit from working and discussing with others?

Some reasons for developing children's ideas about symmetry

Firstly, symmetry is one of the most powerful and intuitive notions in mathematics: 'Being able to call things the "same" is the most powerful mental operation we know, and is, of course, the mainspring of mathematics. It is what enables us to act; and its validity in any particular case is a pragmatic one' (Caldwell 1970:73).

Secondly symmetry has to be experienced. Indeed symmetry or apparent symmetry will already have been experienced to some degree by your pupils; it is part of your role as a mathematics teacher to help pupils appreciate and possibly identify the underlying structures present in many symmetrical configurations. One of the most unfruitful pupil experiences witnessed was listening to a student trying to *explain* bilateral symmetry to a group of 11-year-olds. A much more rewarding experience would be to have children describe what they perceive as 'sameness' or not as the case may be, having had the opportunity to explore some interesting shapes or objects. Small group work which is practically based normally allows for this kind of exploration and at the same time releases the teacher from a central role which allows him/her to join in with the activity and promote discussion within the groups. This combination of child centred activity subtly directed by the teacher allows the development of ideas from *the pupil's* standpoint and not from that of the teacher.'This process has to be seen as one of negotiation of meaning between the teacher and pupils rather than one of imitation by the pupils of what the teacher says' (Brissenden 1988:7).

Thirdly, there is a wealth of materials from which to choose. These can be usefully separated into two groups as follows:

Group A: materials for demonstration
Photographs, particularly of architecture, sculpture and other art forms, and occurrences in nature.
Diagrams.
Everyday objects.
Output from computer programs.
Films and videos.
Books.
Overhead projector and templates.

Group B: materials for pupil workshops
Mirrors.
Tracing paper.
Squared paper.
Templates.
Computer programs.
Books, magazines, workcards.

Finally, there will always be a need to develop your own knowledge and awareness of a particular area of mathematics. This can be done at two levels: from your own level of understanding, and by becoming familiar with various presentations at school level. Pursuing the two together should greatly enhance your own confidence in talking to children.

Concepts of symmetry

Weyl (1952) describes different types of symmetry:

bilateral
translatory
rotational
ornamental/crystallographic.

Much of the work done on symmetry in schools tends to confine itself to bilateral and rotational symmetries and pays little regard to translatory and ornamental symmetries. The latter are to be found in the decorative art of many countries through the ages, and a number of texts listed in the bibliography Davis et al. (1981), Coxeter (1961), Fenn (1930) deal either with the analysis of their structure or with ideas for their construction.

Rosen also broadens the concept of symmetry: 'I cannot find a system to which the concept of symmetry is inapplicable' (1975:6). The broadening of the concept is achieved mainly through the consideration of the symmetry transformations in two and three dimensions. In two dimensions, for example, the concept of glide symmetry is discussed by way of the glide reflection transformation (a combination of a reflection and a translation parallel with the mirror line); in three dimensions, spiral symmetry is produced by a combination of a rotation and a translation as in a spiral staircase. Colour symmetry is also discussed, that is the introduction of colouring or a colour transformation into an existing pattern which produces different symmetries and different possible symmetry transformations. Further discussion of this can be found in MacGillavry (1965).

A note on terminology

It is important whilst discussing mathematics with pupils that correct mathematical language is introduced at the appropriate level and that there is consistency in its use. Important words to be used when discussing symmetry in two and three dimensions are given in Table 2.5 and you should be careful not to mix the two. Many texts, quite wrongly in the author's view, talk about an axis of bilateral symmetry when discussing a planar object.

Table 2.5 **Symmetry terminology**

Symmetry	Two dimensions	Three dimensions
Rotational	Point	Axis
Bilateral	Line	Plane

Rosen (1975) also discusses point symmetry in *three* dimensions, shows that the reflection in a point is equivalent to a rotation, and gives five examples of this as it relates to familiar three-dimensional objects.

Simple programs to illustrate symmetry

Some of the group A materials listed earlier can be used initially to arouse interest and to communicate your own enthusiasm. For example, if you have a microcomputer available the following program, written in BBC Basic, can be loaded (beforehand!) and run to initiate discussion about symmetrical figures. Write down a number of questions you might ask about the images produced. Do not expect formal definitions of the types of symmetry the pupils may see, and try not to confine responses to those relating to aspects of symmetry. Use the responses you receive to widen pupils' interest and to involve them in thinking mathematically. At the least, ideas about 'sameness' should be discussed, and how it manifests itself in the overall pattern and perhaps how it is brought about. By doing this you will not only begin to learn something about the individuals in the group but also ensure that the group builds upon ideas, refines the language used to describe shapes, and decides what is an acceptable form of symmetry.

```
10    MODE2
20    VDU5
30    VDU29,640;520;
40    N=RND(10)
60    PROCkaleido (N)
70    END
80    DEF PROCkaleido (P)
85    Q=0
90    REPEAT
100     FOR L% = 40 TO 500 STEP 20
110       GCOL0,RND(8)-1
120       X% = RND(L%):Y% = RND(X%)
130       X1% = RND(L%):Y1% = RND(X1%)
140       X2% = RND(L%):Y2% = RND(X2%)
150       MOVE X%,Y%: MOVE X1%,Y1%: PLOT 85,X2%,Y2%
160       MOVE -X%,Y%: MOVE -X1%,Y1%: PLOT 85,-X2%,Y2%
170       MOVE X%,-Y%: MOVE X1%,-Y1 PLOT 85,X2%,-Y2%
```

```
180    MOVE  -X%,-Y%:  MOVE  -X1%,-Y1%:  PLOT  85,-X2%,-Y2%
190    MOVE  Y%,X%:  MOVE  Y1%,X1%:  PLOT  85,Y2%,X2%
200    MOVE  -Y%,X%:  MOVE  -Y1%,X1%:  PLOT  85,-Y2%,X2%
210    MOVE  Y%,-X%:  MOVE  Y1%,-X1%:  PLOT  85,Y2%,-X2%
220    MOVE  -Y%,-X%:  MOVE  -Y1%,-X1%:  PLOT  85,-Y2%,-X2%
230   NEXT L%
240   Q = Q+1
250   UNTIL Q = P
260   ENDPROC
```

If you are not acquainted with a programming language, the details of the program and the way it is written need not concern you at this stage. However, if you or the pupils have some knowledge of programming then you could attempt at a later stage to open up the discussion by considering how the picture is drawn, how symmetry is maintained (there is symmetry represented even in the coding: lines 150–220) and possibly how, by changing the coding, symmetry could be destroyed or changed in some way. This particular exercise brings together in a natural way different aspects of mathematics: geometry, algebra, computer programming and problem solving.

Two much shorter programs can be used to produce regular polygons exhibiting both bilateral and rotational symmetries. These are given below and are written in Logotron Logo. One of the benefits of using Logo to study mathematics is that the language (at turtle graphics level) is easily understood and is accessible. The accessibility of the language allows teacher and pupils freedom to experiment with the process for creating designs. This in effect is experimenting with mathematical ideas in an open way which can be so rewarding in terms of building positive attitudes towards learning mathematics. It can also provide a starting point for a more substantial project on symmetry, but more will be said of investigative mathematics later.

```
TO POLY1:SIDE:NUMSIDES
REPEAT:NUMSIDES[FORWARD:SIDE  RIGHT  360/:NUMSIDES]
END


TO POLY2:SIDE:ANGLE
REPEAT 360/:ANGLE[FORWARD:SIDE  RIGHT:ANGLE]
END
```

Examples of calls to these procedures are simply:

```
POLY1 200 7                         POLY2 200 72
```

These are not only easy to type in but also quite easy to understand, even if the pupil's or teacher's experience of programming is limited. The results of the two calls are shown in Figure 2.1. The shape produced by POLY1 has rotational symmetry of order equal to the number of sides typed in as a parameter, and furthermore POLY1 stops

Figure 2.1 **Logo polygon procedures: (a) POLY1 200 7 (b) POLY2 200 72**

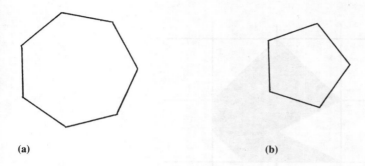

(a)   (b)

after producing the right shape in the minimum number of moves. However, as an illustration of how computers can be useful not only to solve problems but also to pose them, those interested may like to try to produce the same effect as POLY1 200 7 with a call of POLY2. Using a computer to draw these designs will soon make it obvious that the symmetries produced (if any) by the second algorithm are not obvious and greater care has to be taken over the arithmetic thinking and the arithmetic produced by the particular version of Logo. More will be said of the use of Logo in learning about mathematics in Chapter 7.

Short programs such as these can be used effectively as an introduction or to extend pupils' thinking well beyond the introductory stage. If a microcomputer is not available, suitably sized photographs, slides or poster diagrams can also be an effective stimulus for discussion, although they are non-interactive!

Creating patterns with card and paper

This may seem all very well, but what about other activities for a group as a whole? How can we make ideas about symmetry more available to the pupils without losing the visual imagery? One suggestion is to use card templates which can be cheaply and quickly produced by the teacher or the pupils. A simple template can produce quite complicated patterns. The simpler the template the better to begin with. An example follows.

For this demonstration you need: an overhead projector and screen, a square grid overhead transparency, and a number of congruent templates whose vertices coincide with the grid vertices. This will help you to place the pieces precisely so that the pattern produced will have the desired effect.

*Figure 2.2   **Template***

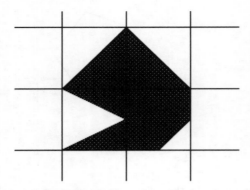

Take the card template shown in Figure 2.2. A number of these templates presented in silhouette can provide a striking and effective way of demonstrating pattern creation; the transformations used to produce such a pattern are continually reinforced as the pattern progresses (Figure 2.3).

*Figure 2.3   **Strip pattern from template***

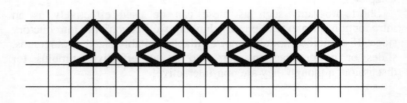

Pattern creation and the techniques for getting there are important factors in motivating pupils and in providing the groundwork for more formally presented work. This particular exercise also provides you with the opportunity of practising your skills with an overhead projector.

Suggested pupil activities

Materials required: a variety of card templates, squared paper, pencils, scissors.

1.   Pupils produce different strip patterns on squared paper using a single card template as a guide. Pupils might also like to produce

their own templates and experiment with them (NC AT11 level 2).

2. Pupils cut out shapes from card and try to 'post' the shape into the hole produced in as many ways as possible:
    (a) by rotating the shape only (NC AT11 level 4)
    (b) by allowing a 'reflection' to take place, simulated by a flip via the third dimension (NC AT11 reinforcing level 3).

    A table can then be produced to record the number of ways of posting with or without a flip and used subsequently to establish the concepts of bilateral symmetry and rotational or point symmetry. All the familiar geometric shapes (square, rectangle, equilateral triangle, parallelogram etc.) can be suggested as starters for this activity, but pupils should also be encouraged to design their own shapes.

Computer generated patterns and friezes

For producing strip patterns, an alternative to the first of the pupil activities in the previous section is to use a computer program. One such program is Newtiles from the Microsmile 2 pack 'The Next 17'. Limited availability of microcomputers may render its use only suitable for extension material. It should be noted that this program is designed to produce tilings in two dimensions and that certain operations or transformations are available (e.g. a rotation of 90°) which are not strictly generators of strip patterns (i.e. they would not leave the whole strip invariant under that transformation; see Coxeter 1961:47–9).

The transformations acting on a basic shape which can be used to produce a strip pattern, that is a pattern which allows translation in one dimension only, and which subsequently leave the strip invariant are:

a translation
a reflection
a half turn
a glide reflection.

These can be combined to produce seven strip patterns, each of which exhibits a distinct symmetry (Figures 2.4–2.10). Using Newtiles, the same basic shape generating each of the strip patterns is shown.

Figure 2.4 **F1: translation**

Figure 2.5 **F2: glide reflection (parallel to direction of strip)**

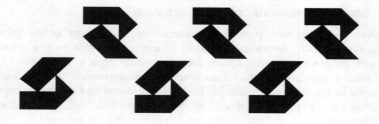

Figure 2.6 **F3: vertical reflection**

Figure 2.7 **F4: half turn**

Figure 2.8 **F5: vertical reflection and half turn**

Figure 2.9 **F6: glide reflection and horizontal reflection**

Figure 2.10 **F7: vertical reflection and horizontal reflection**

Your own investigations into the effects of further combinations of these transformations should enable you to confirm that there are only seven.

For those wishing to follow this theme further, flow charts appear in Crowe (1981). Crowe uses these flow charts to classify patterns found in African art. The first flow chart is for determining the underlying structure in the strip patterns found on decorated pipes in Begho, Ghana. As well as being a device for analysing existing patterns, it could also form the basis of an algorithm for generating one's own strip patterns. A flow chart similar to that appearing in Crowe (1981) for one-dimensional patterns is shown in Figure 2.11.

Figure 2.11 **Flow chart to produce or analyse strip patterns**

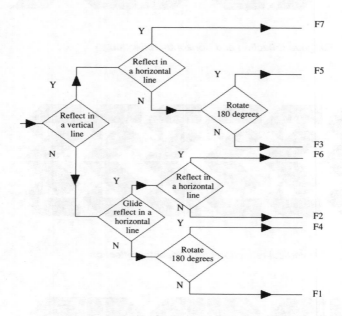

By considering colour change in strip patterns and the operations which bring about these colour changes, three 'new' strip patterns can be generated. These strip patterns are appropriately called Escher friezes, see MacGillavry (1965). It is also possible to produce these friezes using Newtiles, and an example of each using the *same* basic tile design is shown in Figures 2.12–2.13. Figure 2.14 is produced using the same basic title but initially rotated through 90 degrees clockwise. The tile above each frieze shows an intermediate position before the colour change, black to white and white to black, takes place. Readers might like to produce their own basic tile design in order to create Escher friezes.

Figure 2.12 **Escher 1: half turn only, interchanging opposite coloured parts**

Figure 2.13 **Escher 2: glide reflection only, interchanging opposite coloured parts**

Figure 2.14 **Escher 3: either a glide reflection or a half turn, interchanging opposite coloured parts**

Figure 2.15 **Frieze patterns (Fenn 1930)**

A second flow chart in Crowe (1981) is more complicated and is used for classifying two-dimensional designs, of which there are a total of 17. The program Newtiles can also be used to produce some of these patterns; this is best done experimentally in the early stages of the program's use rather than through any attempted analysis of the patterns' underlying structure. Here rotations of 180°, 120°, 90° and 60° are possible, and their combinations with reflections and glide reflections produce the 17 basic designs; however, for rotations only half turns and quarter turns are possible using Newtiles. The analysis of the two-dimensional (wallpaper) patterns and their classification can be an enthralling exercise for the teacher and older pupils. A number of given references deal with this. Cadwell (1966), Coxeter (1961), Davis et al (1981).

Some frieze patterns, typically using glide reflections (Newtiles), are shown in Figure 2.15 (Fenn 1930). Glide reflection patterns are to be found in much of Escher's work (Coxeter *et al*. 1986) and, perhaps surprisingly, in nature: the scaly male fern (*Dryopteris pseudomas*) and the green spleenwort (*Asplenium viride*) provide examples (Phillips 1980: 79, 99). In figure 2.16 glide reflections as well as half-turns produce a wallpaper pattern (Cadwell 1966).

Figure 2.16 **Wallpaper pattern (Cadwell 1966)**

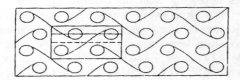

Other resources for teaching symmetry

Software
   Tesselator. (1984) Addison-Wesley
   Maths with a Story. (1985) ILEA.

Simple equipment
   Mirrors.
   Reflectographs.
   Rotograms.
   Compasses.
   Squared paper.
   Triangulated paper.
   Colour symmetry game (E. J. Arnold).
   Hexymmetry set (E. J. Arnold).

Further reading

Ahmed A. 1985 *Mathematics for Low Attainers: Some Classroom Activities and Approaches* West Sussex Institute of Higher Education
Beeney R .1979 Mirror fun *Mathematics Teaching* :33

Bell A., Fletcher T. 1964 *Symmetry Groups* Association of Teachers of Mathematics

Davis C., Grunbaum B., Sherk F. A. (eds) 1981 *The Geometric Vein:the Coxeter Festschrift* Springer, 177–89

Goddijn A. 1980 *Shadow and Depth* IOWO, Utrecht

Mathematics in Action (all books) Blackie-Chambers

Rosen J. 1975 *Symmetry Discovered* Cambridge University Press, Chapter 3

School Mathematics Project (SMP), Books B1 and B2, Booklet 4(e) *Symmetry Tiles*

Walter M. *Readings in Mathematical Education: Geometry* Association of Teachers of Mathematics

Weyl H. 1952 *Symmetry* Princeton University Press

Fractions

The topic of fractions follows as an example of an alternative way of creating an information base in preparation for teaching. Working with fractions is perhaps less appealing than discovering symmetry, but their importance remains as high as ever. They have permeated much of the mathematics curriculum for many years and feature in a number of attainment targets covering key stages 3 and 4 in the National Curriculum; for example AT2 levels 4 and 6, AT3 levels 5, 6 and 7, AT4 level 4, AT5 levels 4 and 7, AT8 levels 3 and 7, and AT14 levels 4 and 5.

At level 4, pupils should be able to recognize and understand simple fractions including the equivalence of fractions. In handling data, pupils are expected to understand and use a probability scale from 0 to 1 and justify in their own way estimates of probabilities. At level 5, pupils should be calculating fractions (or percentages) of quantities, and at level 6 should be able to work out fractional and percentage changes and to *use* equivalence of fractions in calculations.

The teaching and learning of fractions at secondary school level has received a good deal of attention in recent years. The Concepts in Secondary Mathematics and Science (CSMS) project (1974–9) looked at the types of difficulties which children had in a number of areas of the mathematics curriculum, fractions being one of the areas investigated. A sequel to this programme was the Strategies and Errors in Secondary Mathematics (SESM) project (1980–3) Kerslake (1986), which followed up in more detail the nature of the errors revealed by the CSMS project. It would therefore seem prudent for those embarking upon the teaching of fractions to pay some regard to the findings of these two projects.

A widespread cause of error identified by the CSMS project was the lack of understanding of a fraction in any way other than as 'part of a whole'. The CSMS project revealed three particular problems:

1. That many children could not think of a fraction as a number.
2. That a common presentation of a fraction, diagrammatically as part of a whole, has severe limitations on ideas about fractions and operations on fractions.
3. That although children readily identify equivalent fractions they are unable to use equivalence to determine relative sizes or to perform operations on fractions.

The SESM project interviewed a large number of pupils who demonstrated these errors in order to understand the nature of their difficulties, and then ran small scale teaching experiments based on the findings; the ultimate aim was to develop trial material for use with whole classes. Models of fractions, fractions as numbers and equivalent fractions were the main focus of the interviews. It is not possible to do justice here to the rather lengthy report (Kerslake 1986) but I have tried to include some of its findings in my suggestions for teaching fractions.

Models of fractions certainly provide an impressive picture of a whole being divided into equal parts. You will be hard pressed to find a textbook which does not use this approach at some stage. If you look at, for instance, the SMP 11–16 booklet *Fractions 1*, you will find that the whole of the booklet concentrates on models of fractions which emphasize that a fraction is part of a whole, and furthermore the objects used are not normally divided up and displayed as separate distinct pieces. For example, the first picture presented is the Austrian flag (Figure 2.17), of which two-thirds is red and one-third is white. This flag, like any other, is not normally separated into distinct pieces, but rather different areas are seen to link together to form a familiar object. The penultimate problem in the booklet is the more complicated Czechoslovakian flag, which poses essentially the same type of problem. Not until the last question in the booklet, which depicts a pile of eight bricks representing the whole, does the whole become divided up and separated. However, the approach of *Fractions 1* and *2* appeals to pupils' informal knowledge about fractions – knowledge which is based upon their own experience of real life situations – and gradually builds up the symbolic representation of a fraction.

Figure 2.17 **Austrian flag**

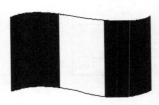

The importance of building upon children's informal knowledge of mathematics is now more recognized. Mack (1990) investigated how the link could be made between pupils' informal knowledge of fractions, their use of fraction symbols and their performance with operations of addition, subtraction and multiplication. There was evidence not only that the teaching of concepts based upon children's informal knowledge supported a meaningful use of algorithms for calculating with fractions, but also that rote learning of such procedures interfered with their attempts to build on such informal knowledge. However, there are clear limitations on the extent to which children are able to draw upon their informal knowledge when presented with fraction problems. In order to understand more clearly the nature of the difficulties related to the teaching of fractions we need to look at a variety of fraction representations.

The widespread, almost exclusive notion of a fraction as part of a whole is probably the result of many textbooks presenting fractions in this way. Other representations of a fraction, for example as a number arising out of division, are less prominent, as are explicit attempts to link concrete representations with their symbolic forms. Kerslake (1986) uses a number of alternative models for fractions in an attempt to discover which models children relate to most. For example, of the eight models of ¾ Figure 2.18, models (a), (b), (d) and (e) were the most widely accepted, closely followed by (g), perhaps because of its closeness to the 'part of a whole' model. The absence of a recognizable whole with model (c) and more so with model (f) caused more children to reject them as representations of ¾. Model (h) was the least popular, many children seeing no connection between 3÷4 and 3/4. However, when they were presented with a familiar activity which involved 'sharing' in a natural way, for example three cakes shared equally by four children, most children could see the connection.

Figure 2.18 **Models for 3/4 (Kerslake 1986)**

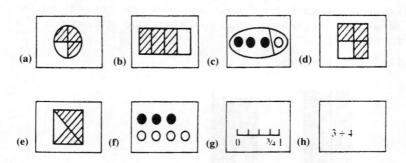

Clearly the way in which we represent fractions and place them in context can influence how children begin to think about them. The notion of a fraction as a (rational) number, less than or greater than unity, which is unrelated to a problem situation or a representative model is beyond the normal experience of many children in the early years of secondary school. It would appear, in the light of this knowledge of children's difficulties, that a scheme of work extending across the early years of secondary school should include attempts to broaden children's concept of a fraction. Such attempts should include not only a variety of representations of fractions and problems which require and generate the use of fractions, but also the pupil–pupil and pupil–teacher interaction necessary for ideas about fractions to develop in a meaningful way.

The SESM project (Kerslake 1986) attempted to challenge children's ideas about fractions by encouraging the children to work in pairs or small groups in order to discuss fraction 'problems' presented to them in a series of worksheets. They focused upon the difficulties already mentioned. A few examples follow which are taken from the tests. From these examples and the discussion it is hoped that you will be able to devise or select your own fraction problems for pupils known to you.

The first two examples are simple illustrations:

1. The 2 pints of milk in Figure 2.19 are divided equally between the 3 cups. How much milk is there in each cup?
2. 3 pints of water in Figure 2.20 are divided equally between the 2 jugs. How much water is there in each jug?

Figure 2.19 **Fractions problem (Kerslake 1986)**

Figure 2.20 **Fractions problem (Kerslake 1986)**

These two examples illustrate that thinking about fractions can begin without the need for skills in symbolic manipulation; they both appeal to a child's experience and informal knowledge. They also invoke the *idea* of division of one number by another; that is, $2 \div 3$ and $3 \div 2$ taken together challenge the ideas that on the one hand all fractions are necessarily less than unity, and on the other hand a number divided by a larger number gives a value of zero, instilled by saying '3 goes into 2 zero times.'

Calculator use was also encouraged to determine the results of $1 \div 2$, $1 \div 4$, $3 \div 4$ etc. and to compare these decimal fraction results with their fraction equivalents ½, ¼, ¾ etc. (Note that calculators which allow an input in fraction form will normally convert this to a decimal fraction when it is entered into memory.) This use of a calculator lends itself readily to the idea of equivalence: for example it is easy to test for the equivalence of ¼, ⅛, ⁵⁄₂₀ etc., and to reinforce at the same time the 'equivalence' of $1 \div 4$, $2 \div 8$, $5 \div 20$ etc.

Two further equivalence ideas were used. One was in word problem form: a fixed amount was shared firstly between three people, two of whom received equal amounts and secondly between four people where each person received a different amount. Ideas about equivalent and non-equivalent fractions were invoked. The other compared fractions for size or equivalence using number lines (Figure 2.21).

Figure 2.21 **Fractions using number lines (Kerslake 1986)**

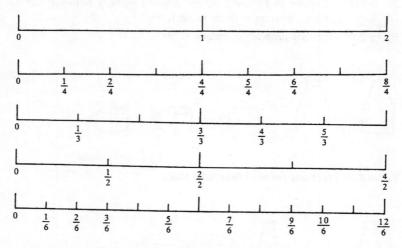

This approach not only has an automatic appeal when dealing with equivalence but also illustrates the idea that fractions can be represented by points on a number line, i.e. that a fraction is a number and the relative sizes of these numbers can be compared. Addition of fractions can follow in a more natural way, for example $\frac{3}{4}+\frac{1}{8}$ = $\frac{6}{8}+\frac{1}{8}$ = $\frac{7}{8}$ using Figure 2.22. Similarly, $\frac{1}{3}+\frac{1}{2}$ = $\frac{2}{6}+\frac{3}{6}$ = $\frac{5}{6}$ can be calculated by linking each fraction to its equivalent fraction in sixths. This way attempts to *use* equivalence in the addition of fractions.

Figure 2.22 **Addition of fractions**

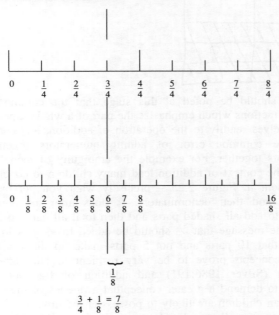

$$\frac{3}{4} + \frac{1}{8} = \frac{7}{8}$$

In later work by Hart *et al.* (1989) it was found that although equivalent fractions could be adequately represented in diagram form as part of a whole, children often could not demonstrate that they understood equivalence by drawing appropriate diagrams, even though they thought they could. For example $\frac{3}{4}$ would be drawn as in Figure 2.23 but $\frac{6}{8}$ as in Figure 2.24.

Figure 2.23 **Children's representation of 3/4 (Hart et al. 1989)**

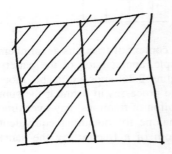

Figure 2.24 **Children's representation of 6/8 (Hart et al. 1989)**

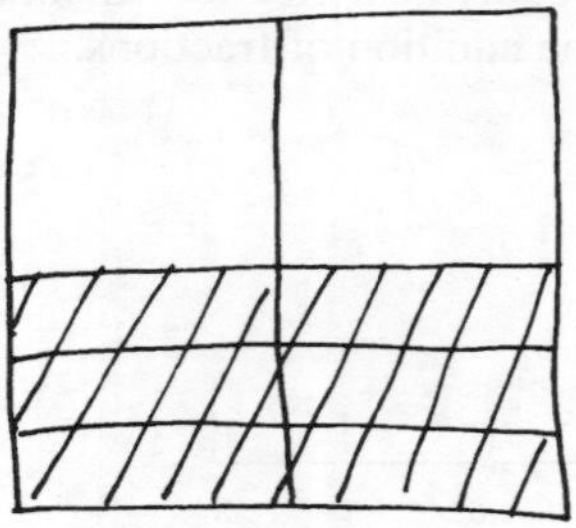

Also it should be noted at this stage that the commonly used models of fractions which emphasize the part of a whole aspect do not lend themselves readily to the operation of addition, and can in fact support the common error of adding numerators together and denominators together. For example the ambiguity of models for 3/5 and 1/5 in the context of addition lead many children to conclude that 4/10 is present in Figure 2.25 – precisely what you get by adding numerators and then denominators. It does after all seem quite reasonable to add all shaded parts and then total all parts to form the fraction. The message that 3/5 should be added to 1/5 gets lost in the perception that 10 parts and not 5 parts make up the whole. Such erroneous concepts prove to be very resilient to later attempts at remediation (Silver 1986:191) and addition of fractions is now considered to demand a greater conceptual awarenes of the nature of fractions than children are likely to possess at the time when addition of fractions is normally taught. However, the research by Mack (1990) does suggest that such a modelling can offer children a meaningful approach which can be extended, provided that the link between their informal knowledge and fraction symbols is 'reasonably clear'.

Figure 2.25 **Ambiguity in fractions addition**

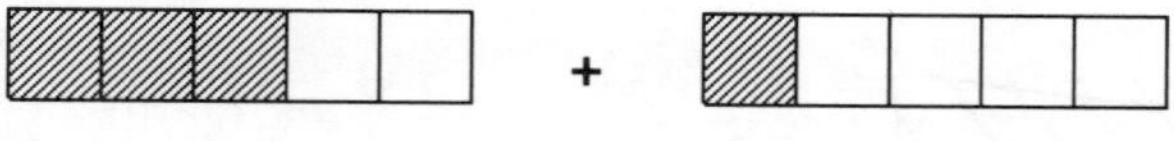

Multiplication of fractions set in the context of fractions as numbers is a more achievable target. For example, appreciation of the pattern for multiplication established by Figure 2.26 appears to be more achievable than an understanding of the processes in forming the sum 1/3 + 1/2. Such experiences in multiplication of fractions may over time provide sufficient contrast to the technique for obtaining equivalent fractions by multiplying top and bottom of a fraction by the same

Figure 2.26 **Multiplication of fractions**

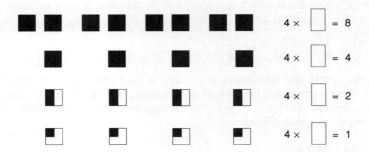

number. It would be a test of the development of pupils' conceptual knowledge of equivalent fractions whether they thought such operations increased the fraction or left it unaltered. If this method of obtaining equivalent fractions is pursued you should be careful not to use the instruction 'what you do to the top you must do to the bottom.' You will find that children need no encouragement to add or subtract the same values from top and bottom of a fraction thus:

$$\frac{6}{8} = \frac{6-2}{8-2} = \frac{4}{6}$$

Any explanation of why this is not so is likely to be beyond the conceptual awareness of most pupils. The awareness that multiplication (or division) preserves the ratio, whereas addition (or subtraction) does not, comes much later in a pupil's thinking – and in some cases not at all.

Another aspect of coping with fractions not reported by Kerslake (1986) or Hart *et al.* (1989) is to abandon their conventional notation (see van Hiele 1986 : 215). This may seem a rather drastic step to take, but careful use of a calculator which has a facility for representing reciprocals (x^{-1}) rather than fractions (a/b) allows most of the basic numeric ideas about fractions to be explored without the cognitive overload often present when children try to cope with difficult conceptual and procedural aspects of traditionally written fractions. It should be said that I am not aware of this being tried for any length of time; moreover, replacing ⅖ by 2×5^{-1} for example may remove difficult concepts of division and denominators but may also introduce new difficulties, not least in accepting the new form of fraction. As far as testing for equivalence or relative size of fractions goes this representation lends itself rather well. For example, in testing which is the greater of ⅚ and ⅞, one way would be to simply try each on a calculator entered either as fractions or in the form 5×6^{-1} and

7×8^{-1}. However, the latter form allows us to multiply each fraction by 6×8 giving 40 and 42 respectively, indicating with the possibility of some understanding, that ⅞ is the greater. The numbers 40 and 42 are precisely those which are generated by the widely used addition of fractions algorithm, i.e.

$$\frac{5}{6} + \frac{7}{8} = \frac{40 + 42}{48} = \frac{82}{48}$$

if we ignore the refinement of finding a least common denominator. One could argue that the following algorithm, which 'moves the space' to numbers 48 times bigger, is conceptually more accessible and removes the need for division:

$$(5 \times 6^{-1}) + (7 \times 8^{-1})$$

rewritten as $(5 \times 6^{-1} \times 6 \times 8) + (7 \times 8^{-1} \times 6 \times 8) = 40 + 42 = 82$

The concept of division can be left while this stage is reached. Since the resulting number is 48 times too big, division by 48 is necessary; hence 82⁄48 is an acceptable answer form. This appears to have possibilities as an alternative technique; it has the merit of having a plausible explanation. It is also arguable that if the calculations are done using a calculator then the number 1.7083 will have more meaning than 1¹⁷⁄24, however use of a calculator is likely to result in a different method of calculation. Certainly numbers like the former are more likely to occur in working environments of today.

In summary, there appears to be a strong case for delaying the use of fraction symbols and techniques for operating on fractions until links between a pupil's informal knowledge of fractions and their symbolic representation are made manifestly clear. It is advocated to adopt a broad and varied approach to the concept of fractions using calculators and number lines, and to pursue a teaching style which allows children to discuss with each other their own ideas about fractions.

This chapter has attempted to highlight some of the needs and pupil difficulties which the inexperienced teacher is likely to meet. There are many topics which in your role as teacher you may be asked to prepare and teach. The discussions relating to preparing to teach symmetry and preparing to teach fractions are illustrative of how you may go about such preparations regarding the underlying content and curricular knowledge. Further areas of content and curricular knowledge are discussed in Chapter 3 in the context of individual lesson planning or of planning to use published mathematics schemes.

Effective approaches to the teaching of mathematics

'It is not altogether impossible that even an average teacher using this kind of textbook [colourless] and implementing a theory of his own does better than a good teacher who is bound to a textbook of a character that does not match the character of his own teaching'. . . . instruction is probably better than its textbooks. (Freudenthal 1973: 159, 160)

With this mixture of caveat and optimism well noted, an overview of some of the developments in the mathematics curriculum in Britain is attempted with specific references to schemes for secondary mathematics which are currently in widespread use. The aim is to raise the consciousness of the inexperienced teacher to these influences upon how teachers teach and how children learn.

It is unlikely that a student on teaching practice will be in a position to come to terms with the plethora of material which has entered Britain's schools over the last few years. Much of this material is designed to assist teachers to make what are regarded as very necessary changes to not only *what* mathematics we can expect pupils to learn and how much of it there should be for certain abilities but also *how* these tasks in general terms might be approached. It is evident from publications on mathematics teaching from such bodies as the Department of Education and Science (DES) and the Schools Examinations and Assessment Council (SEAC) (England and Wales), and the Scottish Office Education Department (SOED), Scottish Examination Board (SEB) and the Scottish Consultative Council on the Curriculum (Scotland), that the *what, how much* and *by when for whom* are relatively easy to define in terms of profile components and attainment targets. The route by which all this might be achieved is not so easily drawn, although as early as 1982 the Cockcroft Report as it now relates to these criteria gave a glimpse of what was to come:

Research shows that these three – facts and skills, conceptual structures, general strategies and appreciation – involve distinct aspects of teaching and require separate attention. It follows that effective mathematics teaching must pay attention to all three. (DES 1982: paragraph 241)

These ideas continued to be aired in the proposals for a national curriculum in mathematics (DES 1988), typically as:

In planning their schemes of work, teachers should select topics which between them cover all aspects of mathematics defined by the attainment targets . . . It is important that each topic is carefully analysed to ensure that there is a match between the mathematical possibilites offered and the mathematical knowledge, skills and understanding which each child is ready to meet. (DES 1988: 64)

I do not want to read too much into just two extracts from these reports, but together they seem to reflect a trend in mathematics teaching that many in the field of mathematics education regard as very desirable. In the quotation from the Cockcroft Report there is a linking of 'distinct aspects of teaching' to desirable outcomes, and further paragraphs of the report go on to spell out what these distinct aspects are. In the quotation from the national curriculum proposals there is a more apparent awareness of the importance of where the child's abilities with mathematics lie in relation to what is being taught. The importance of this matching continued to be developed, culminating in *Mathematics in the National Curriculum* (DES 1989) as programmes of study which are linked to ten attainment levels. These represent not only a nationally recognized entitlement but a clear reference for raising the minimum levels of expectation and progress from 5 to 16.

It is in this regard that the mathematics schemes which allow a considerable amount of individual and small group work appear to have their greatest strength. It is quite possible now for teachers to create within an existing framework 'individual' programmes of work for each child in the class. Both the Kent Mathematics Project (KMP) and the Smile scheme make use of networks which contain mathematical topics at steadily increasing concept levels. There is also some variation in the mode of presentation. Various routes through the networks are devised by the teacher/'manager' which, within the bounds of the project, relate to where the child is mathematically and where over a number of weeks the same child can progress to. Progression normally takes place across a number of mathematical topics specified by means of a pupil matrix of tasks which can be taken, with a few exceptions, in any order. Effectively this provides a number of mathematical tasks which the pupil has to experience either working alone or working with a partner or partners.

This approach certainly provides the action required to move pupils from an all too often passive position of receiving the perceived wisdom of the teacher to a position where, in theory, they have to think largely for themselves. However, reference to Skemp's (1971) building of schemata readily shows that this consciousness raising stage, when many new concepts begin to be formed, requires more than just experience with material. What is experienced often needs to be shared with other pupils, and the continued development of ideas gained from these experiences will be best brought about through discussion with other pupils or the teacher. The refinement of ideas brought about in a dynamic way through challenge, partial agreement and dispute cannot be substituted by even the most carefully written workcard. 'The more solutions and strategies pupils see and discuss, the more likely they are to develop a real appreciation of mathematics at their own level' (Ahmed 1987: 17).

There is a great temptation for the young teacher to allow any adopted scheme to dominate how topics are presented and developed, which in turn inhibits any arrangement which encourages pupils to test their ideas against others or to reflect on their experiences. The teacher's time is consumed at worst in attending to the strictly managerial organizational role, and often at best in dealing with the immediate problems of helping highly motivated pupils through the next set of tasks presented by the system. 'Mathematics is effectively learned only by experimenting, questioning, reflecting, discovering, inventing and discussing' (Ahmed 1987: 16). Any use of a system which denies pupils the opportunity for reflection, discussion and the posing of their own questions must be seriously questioned.

For the inexperienced teacher there is also the added danger which a large diet of running such commercially produced schemes brings. Firstly, there is a tendency not to do mathematics for one's own sake, and not to read a number of varied accounts and presentations, and not to discuss with colleagues in order to develop one's own ideas about a topic – ideas through which the teacher can often convey his/her interest and enthusiasm for mathematics. Secondly, the overuse of such schemes removes or drastically reduces the much needed opportunities to practise the whole group communication skills so essential to the all round development of the teacher. Thirdly, such schemes, if allowed to, inhibit the ways in which the activities of a lesson can be structured. Pedagogical experimentation followed by careful evaluation is another casualty. Fourthly, there can be a filtering out of the personal view of mathematics which good teachers normally bring to lessons. The personality of the teacher and his/her relationship with mathematics can become shrouded by repetitive overindulgent superficial activity.

This is a plea for moderation in the use of such schemes, particularly where inexperienced teachers are in a position of needing to acquire and develop basic skills very quickly. How then should the young teacher plan lessons when such schemes are in use? What strategies can be attempted so that the experience of a combination of whole class teaching and individualized or small group work can be used to best effect in a teacher's early development? I will attempt to answer in part these questions in the hope that students who may be faced with using mathematics schemes for the first time, possibly during a first teaching practice, can plan more effectively.

Lesson Planning

During the period prior to a first teaching practice you will no doubt have discussed many educational issues with your tutors and other students, and having observed classes or taken part in microteaching sessions you will have formulated some ideas about how you see yourself in a classroom working with children. You will also have some new or refreshed ideas about how to go about creating situations in which mathematics can be learned. Coming to terms with the reality of a first timetable can be a daunting task, and the preparation necessary to cope adequately with the variety of content and approach and with different pupil abilities is likely to test even the most gifted student. As well as attempting to satisfy the real needs of your pupils, a first priority, you may also feel a need to satisfy the class teacher and your tutor that your preparation is sound. Schools using an established mathematics scheme which allows individual programmes of study to be made often arrange for fixed periods within the week when whole class, topic-based lessons can be taught using traditional textbooks and materials. In many secondary schools this is an established pattern of working, particularly in the first two years, and it provides the student with the opportunity for planning whole class lessons for younger pupils. For whole class, topic-based lessons a single format using appropriate subheadings will largely suffice. A typical format for planning such lessons is as follows:

topic
age and ability range of pupils
duration
knowledge assumed
materials required
objectives
introduction
development
organization/activity
summary
evaluation.

Certain aspects of this kind of lesson plan may seem a bit of a chore, particularly as you become more familiar with procedures and gain in confidence. However, it has to be borne in mind that systematic planning not only helps to develop your own potential but also provides a day to day account of your teaching activities for those who are concerned for your development as a teacher. For example, the small detail of providing the dates on which lessons were given can take on much more significance for the tutor or class teacher when an overall picture of progress is required. Given this or similar formats and the appropriate variation in content, such lessons can provide the necessary basis for developing your skills as a whole class teacher. The following sections expand on aspects of the lesson plan.

Introducing the lesson

Despite what was said earlier about students' tendencies to concentrate on good beginnings, sometimes at the expense of careful planning of the body of the lesson, planning for a good beginning is nevertheless an important part of planning for the whole lesson. Seven activities which can be usefully employed to begin a lesson have been identified by Runion and are listed in Travers *et al.* (1977):

1. Stating goals: this has already been covered in the discussion on objectives or learning outcomes in Chapter 2.
2. Outlining: a simple strategy where the main points of the lesson are given usually in written form.
3. Use of analogues: a process of relating a new topic to pupils' experiences through something which is familiar to them.
4. Using historical material: relating a problem in the history of mathematics to the topic about to be taught.
5. Reviewing previous related work: reviewing directly related knowledge, skills or understanding. This is often overused as a start to a lesson.
6. Giving reasons: this could lead to difficulties and, if used, reasons need to be short and to the point.
7. Presenting a situation: this is becoming increasingly used as a start to investigative work in mathematics.

These can be used in combination, but any one will set the scene for a lesson and place the mathematics to be learned in a context. Each is now discussed further.

Stating objectives or learning outcomes for the lesson

Unless the lesson is designed to be a discovery lesson or in some cases an open problem-solving lesson, there seems little to be gained by not telling pupils what the intentions of the lesson are. However, your intentions should be conveyed in a simple concise way and you should be careful to use language which pupils can understand. The specific learning outcomes may relate to all or just one of the areas identified in *Mathematics 5–14* as 'problem solving and enquiry skills', 'concepts, facts and techniques', and 'attitudes, awareness and personal qualities'. They may relate to content or process or both. Some specific objectives as they relate to the teaching of symmetry and relevant attainment targets are given in Chapter 2.

Outlining the main points of the lesson in written form

This may serve a number of purposes. Firstly, in its more obvious sense, it allows pupils to see the structure of the lesson which is removed from the actual learning situation. Secondly, it allows you, the teacher, to identify key areas for development; this sets the scene for the learning tasks and activities of the lesson. Thirdly, the outline could form the basis of a summary of the lesson in bringing the lesson to a close.

The following are given as examples. The first might be considered an outline, the second more of a summary. The topic under consideration is 'solving a simple linear equation which has fractional coefficients'.

Outline

1. The idea of equivalent equations:
    (a) equivalent equations which do not involve fractions,
        e.g. $2x - 6 = 0$ and $3 - x = 0$
    (b) equivalent equations where one containing fractions is converted to a simpler form, e.g. $2 - x/3 = 1$ converted to $6 - x = 3$
    (c) use of graphics to illustrate how the equations share the same solution.
2. Techniques for finding equivalent equations:
    (a) determine LCM of denominators
    (b) multiply each term in the equation by this LCM
    (c) take care with signs and any brackets present.

Summary

1. Equations which have the same solution can be called equivalent equations. For example, $2x - 6 = 0$ and $3 - x = 0$ have the same solution $x = 3$.
2. Equations which look quite different can be equivalent. For example, $2 - x/3 = 1$ and $6 - x = 3$ are equivalent and have the same solution. The first can be changed to the second by multiplying each term on both sides of the equation by 3, the only denominator in the equation.
3. Where there is more than one denominator, find the LCM of these and again multiply each term of the equation by this number. For example, in $x/2 - 2 = x/3$ the denominators have an LCM of 6, multiplying through by 6 gives $3x - 12 = 2x$; hence $x = 12$.

Using an analogue

As Polya (1945) says, if we can find an analogue this is good news. This was said in the context of problem solving but clearly the approach has value here. If our aim is to introduce an unfamiliar part of the syllabus and we know of some applicable analogue then it makes sense to explore its relevance. As well as using it to promote the individual lesson we are also demonstrating implicitly its use in mathematical thinking in a wider sense. In a way we have already used an analogue in the outline above. We illustrated by means of two simple equations how one equation can be 'converted' to another; the presence of fractions in the equation is not enough to make the analogue invalid. In other words we recognize that the *system* is the same.

The following are examples of the use of mathematical analogies:

1. Modelling the idea of a composite function. It is assumed that pupils will be familiar with function notation. For example, given $f(x) = x - 2$ and $g(x) = 3x$, then the idea behind $f(g(x)) = 3x - 2$ and $g(f(x)) = 3(x - 2)$ can be expressed in terms of two function machines where the output of the first becomes the input for the second (Figure 3.1).

Figure 3.1 **Representations of (a) f(g(x)) = 3x – 2 (b) g(f(x)) = 3(x–2)**

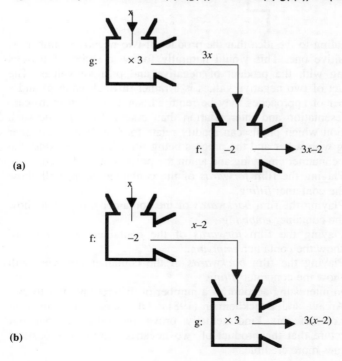

(a)

(b)

2. Meeting negative numbers for the first time. Simple ideas about a stairway above and below ground are very effective. For example, starting at stair 5 and descending 8 stairs is an equivalent system to performing 5–8. The result is 3 stairs below ground, equivalent to negative 3 (Figure 3.2).

Figure 3.2 **Staircase to illustrate negative numbers**

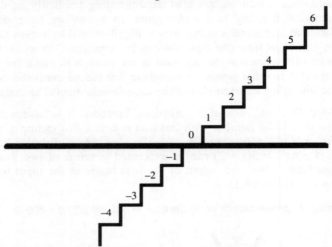

3. Appealing to the idea that the product of two negative numbers is a positive one. This would naturally follow a series of lessons dealing with the product of negative and positive values. The product of two negative values is a rather difficult concept and a number of approaches may be required, some needing more care in presentation and interpretation than others. Here is one such situation which pupils can readily relate to. Consider a container filling with water and the process being filmed. Now consider the same container emptying and again the process being filmed.
    (a) Playing the film *forwards* of the container *filling* will show the container *filling*.
    (b) Playing the film *backwards* of the container *filling* will show the container *emptying*.
    (c) Playing the film *forwards* of the container *emptying* will show the container *emptying*.
    (d) Playing the film *backwards* of the container *emptying* will show the container *filling*.
    For an interesting account of a number of different models to use, see Arcavi and Bruckheimer (1981). Of course no number of instances of this kind actually prove the outcome, but our conjecture that the product of two negative numbers is positive becomes more credible.

Using historical material

Clearly it will not always be possible or desirable to identify relevant material which has strong historical connections. Books on the history of mathematics tend to be rather difficult to read, let alone copies of original manuscripts. There will be occasions however when suitable material can be found. I give one example which also develops the idea of analogy.

Geometry was the major innovation of the Greeks. Significant contributions continued for more than three centuries. Names which readily spring to mind are Euclid, Pythagoras, Apollonius and Archimedes. It is surprising that the use of just the rule and compass was sufficient to sustain their geometry for so long. A less well known Greek mathematician was Hippocrates of Chios, not to be confused with the more celebrated physician, who discovered around 430 BC that if certain plane figures were bounded by circular arcs then a simple relationship between the area of the figure and the area contained between the arcs could be found. This, so far as I am aware, has found no practical use. However, a related problem of 'squaring the circle', that is of constructing a square of area equal to that of a given circle, has attracted considerable attention throughout the ages; although no solution using Euclidean tools is possible, the search has nevertheless led to many other discoveries.

Hippocrates' first theorem states that if a semicircle is drawn on the hypotenuse of an isosceles right-angled triangle so that it passes through the vertex, and another semicircle is drawn on one of the other sides, then the area between the arcs, known as a lune, is equal to half the area of the triangle (Figure 3.3).

*Figure 3.3 **Hippocrates' theorem: area B = (1/2) area A***

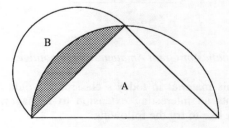

Consequently if a semicircle is drawn on the remaining side then the area of both lunes equals the area of the triangle (Figure 3.4).

Figure 3.4 **Hippocrates' theorem: area B + area C = area A**

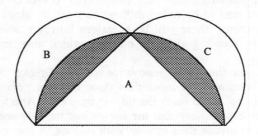

Much later Leonardo da Vinci (1452–1519) of Florence found this of great interest. In addition to painting, he invented many things from paddle wheels for boats to pointed bullets for ammunition, but so far as is known he did not use directly his many drawings which related to this theorem in any of his inventions. One of Leonardo's drawings is shown in Figure 3.5.

Figure 3.5 **A drawing by Leonardo da Vinci (Coolidge 1990)**

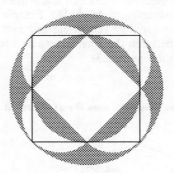

From the Mathematics of Great Amateurs, J L Coolidge

The use of this material in today's classroom would appear valid since it represents an interesting extension to Pythagoras' theorem. The reader might like to try the following:

1. Develop your own ideas for presenting Hippocrates' theorem to a class.
2. Generalize Hippocrates' theorem and develop an analogy with Pythagoras' theorem.

3. Given that the radius of the circle inside the square is 1, deduce that the total area of the unshaded parts in Figure 3.5 is 4.
4. Design some 'luney' shapes for yourself and devise some questions about them.

Reviewing previous related work

This method of starting a lesson predominates, possibly because material is to hand and it is relatively easy to prepare. However, such reviews should be informed by good practice which takes account of pupil difficulties from previous lessons and the hierarchical nature of the mathematics within the given topic, for example knowing how to scale a graph before using it to present information.

The following general points should be remembered:

1. Be clear in your own mind what it is that pupils should know before proceeding.
2. Determine their level of understanding – mainly by questioning.
3. Allow pupils to express their own doubts and difficulties.
4. Be prepared to use in combination with this approach the other ways suggested in this section.

Giving reasons

It is thought that giving reasons for studying a particular topic helps to develop an initial interest and some motivation to look further into the mathematics. As I have already indicated this could easily lead to difficulties. Part of the problem of making a success of this approach is that although you may be quite sure of your reasons, convincing pupils may not be easy. Consequently there is some danger that what is designed to be a good start to a lesson becomes a rather protracted and difficult start. Clearly certain topics are more easily explained from a utilitarian point of view, e.g. percentages, fractions, and project work on aspects of daily finance or planning holidays. But what reasons would you give for studying Hippocrates' theorem? After all, there has been little use made of this since the fourth century BC.

Presenting a situation

This type of start to a lesson gives the teacher the opportunity to develop problem-solving skills on a whole class basis even though some of the subsequent activity could be in small groups or pairs. It differs from the type of situations presented by a workcard scheme in that there is an opportunity for the teacher to control the events taking place across the whole class since there is a common goal. Controlling events does not mean closing down a situation, which leads to a premature end, but rather means broadening a situation by asking open-ended questions which have no clear or immediate answer. This kind of approach should encourage a more open working relationship between teacher and pupil where both can be seen to come to terms with the situation and perhaps to have been wrong in their initial assessments. More of this is said in Chapter 4.

Games can provide rich situations for problem solving. One such game which involves throwing dice is suggested in the *NCTM Yearbook 1981*. It is a game I have often used with students for developing their ideas about probability. It is described briefly below.

An important point to remember when starting a situation-led lesson is to present the situation clearly and concisely. In this case presenting the rules of the game so that play can begin quickly is important if you are to reach the goal of thinking about probabilities. Rules such as these can be presented on handouts or by using an overhead projector. They are as follows:

1.   Each player has a 3 x 3 square array.
2.   A throw may use one, two, three or four dice.
3.   After each throw the total appearing must be entered somewhere in the array and not subsequently moved.
4.   In order to score: a row must be an addition sum (left to right); a column must be a subtraction sum (downwards); a diagonal must be a multiplication sum (downwards).

Figure 3.6 gives an indication of some of the possibilities. Deciding on a fair scoring system for such a set of rules can provide another source for group discussion.

Figure 3.6 **Dice game example**

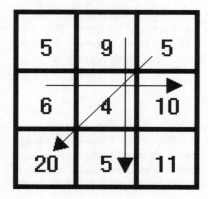

At each turn there are two basic decisions to be made:

1. How many dice are to be thrown?
2. Where should the resultant number be placed?

Here the situation eventually creates the need to know something more about the probabilities of getting a certain score. Some decisions are clear cut, others are open to intuition; but some, for example maximizing our chances of throwing a total of 13, are not so obvious. A fuller account of the use of a spreadsheet to determine probabilities can be found in Simmons (1990).

Developing and completing the lesson

The next consideration for whole class lessons is the development of the chosen introduction. If an outline is prepared as suggested earlier this can certainly act as a guide in planning how the lesson can proceed. There is a danger however that, in coming to terms with content, organization, kinds of activities and other constraints, you will lose sight of the purposes of the lesson. Two important questions to ask yourself at this stage are:

1. What should pupils learn from the lesson?
2. How will I know what they have learnt?

Keeping sight of these two questions will help you to maintain a focus for the lesson and help you to organize appropriate learning activities. In turn this will determine your choice of classroom organization and the type of materials required. Asking the second question, 'How will I know what they have learnt?', will force you into considering how to monitor and evaluate pupils' progress. Only in this way can you assess objectively the success of your lessons.

Clearly presentation of a lesson and its monitoring are closely linked. If, for example, we take the role of questioning in developing a lesson, it not only affects how the lesson will develop but affords a continuing monitoring process as the lesson unfolds. The number and type of questions asked will also affect the quality of your lessons. Questions during the planning stage can be linked to outlines in the sense that their position in your planned sequence reflects the key points of the lesson, and the appropriate use of questions underlines the importance of these key issues and at the same time provides vital feedback from pupils. Rarely is one question sufficient, and your planning should show a certain amount of anticipation and flexibility by noting down possible question sequences which probe the understanding of pupils. Open demand questions are likely to promote more thought about content than closed questions which merely seek information. Both have a role to play but it is important to realize that their use has a different effect on pupils' thinking and their responses. (See Bloom's taxonomy of cognitive processes in Chapter 4, and discussion in the classroom in Chapter 5.)

Another aspect of lesson planning which is part of both presentation and monitoring is the choice of activity, which may be anything from group work using materials and teacher designed worksheets to whole class exercises from an established textbook. If you genuinely choose your own learning outcomes for the lesson then at least a compromise between these two extremes may be necessary. To use a class textbook uncritically under these circumstances may provide neither the learning experiences you really want nor quality control of these experiences.

Lesson summaries provide the necessary drawing together of the main points of the lesson. Many can be planned for, but you should also be flexible enough to incorporate new contributions made by the class in the process of the lesson. This indicates that you value their findings and are prepared to put them alongside your own. In order to make the best use of this part of the lesson, sufficient time should be allowed for it to take place in an unhurried manner. There is little to be gained by rushing through a list of key points while pupils are more interested in packing away their belongings.

Lesson evaluation proves to be a demanding exercise for the student teacher. I have seen many which, despite advice to the contrary, contain only descriptions of the work of one or two individuals and the difficulties they may have had. This of course has some relevance, but in order to get an overall impression of a whole class activity you have to go back to the original lesson objectives and decide whether you observed the majority of the class succeeding at the set tasks and under what conditions this success was achieved. In effect you are asking 'Where are we now?' in order to ask the subsequent question 'Where next?' Some indication of your own performance should also be given: a change of emphasis, a change of introduction, more searching questions, a change in level of difficulty, and so on.

Lesson plan example

Topic

Area, Pythagoras, Hippocrates.

Age and Ability of pupils

Pupils age 14–15, of average and above average ability.

Duration

1 hour 20 minutes.

Knowledge assumed

Pythagoras' theorem.
Area of a circle.
Mathematical similarity.

Materials required

Rulers, compasses, exercise books, plain paper, worksheet.

Objectives

(a) Content

To consolidate pupils' understanding of Pythagoras' theorem and to apply it in unfamiliar circumstances (NCAT 10 level 7).

To develop the idea of similarity and scale factor in an unfamiliar situation. (NCAT 11 levels 7,8).

To broaden pupils' appreciation of plane geometry by bringing in a historical perspective.

To consolidate area of a circle.

To introduce the idea of a lune and its relationship with circles and triangles (Hippocrates' theorem).

To encourage deductive thinking.

(b) Process

To design shapes containing lunes.
To pose questions relating to areas in each shape produced.

Introduction

Historical material similar to that given earlier, presented orally with overheads listing key names and dates, diagrams and possibly photographs.

Overhead transparency diagrams to include 'standard' Pythagoras' theorem (Figure 3.7a) and variants and Hippocrates' theorem (Figure 3.7b).

Figure 3.7 *(a)Pythagoras' theorem (b)Hippocrates' theorem*

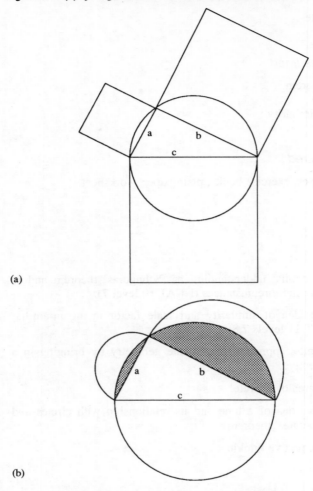

(a)

(b)

Overhead transparency diagrams of similar shapes: squares, similar quadrilaterals, similar triangles, semicircles, similar segments.

Development

By questioning, draw attention to the *similarity* of the squares in the familiar theorem. Possibly use separate diagrams to place squares and other similar shapes side by side (similar triangles, similar rectangles etc.) and determine through questioning the nature of their similarity. Be prepared to draw on counter-examples to show non-similarity (e.g. non-similar rectangles).

Use more similar shapes and place on the side of a right-angled triangle to illustrate analogues of Pythagoras' theorem (Figure 3.8). Make the generalization $kc^2 = ka^2 + kb^2$, where k is a scale factor.

Make the connection between Pythagoras' theorem and Hippocrates' theorem.

Figure 3.8 **Analogues of Pythagoras' theorem: $kc^2 = ka^2 + kb^2$**

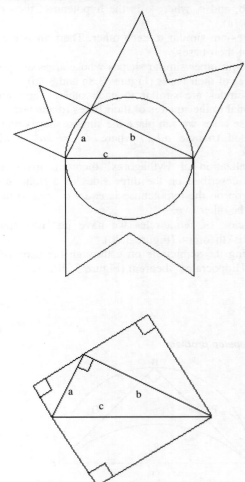

(a)

(b)

Organization/activity

Whole class working from overhead transparencies and prepared worksheet. Worksheet to contain sufficient diagrams, questions and explanations to lead from what is familiar to what is less familiar, gradually encouraging pupils to pose their own problems related to the quadrature of patterns of lunes (e.g. Figure 3.5).

Summary

1. Pythagoras' theorem states that given a right-angled triangle with sides a, b, and c, where c is the hypotenuse, then $c^2 = a^2 + b^2$ (Figure 3.7a).
2. All squares are similar to each other. Their areas are equal to the squares of their bases.
3. We can form other similar shapes whose areas are proportional to the squares of their bases (Figures 3.8a and 3.8b).
4. All semicircles are similar to each other. Their areas are also proportional to the squares of their bases (diameters).
5. In all these cases we can place the similar shapes on the sides of a right-angled triangle a,b,c, where $kc^2 = ka^2 + kb^2$ for some positive k.
6. A generalization of Pythagoras' theorem: given three similar polygons described on the three sides of a right-angled triangle, the polygon on the hypotenuse is equal in area to the sum of the areas of the other two.
7. For the case of semicircles we have just one special case of Pythagoras' theorem. (Figure 3.7b).
8. By drawing the semicircle on c through the apex of the triangle we have Hippocrates' theorem (Figure 3.7b).

Extension

Figure 3.9 **Extension problem**

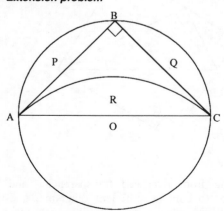

In Figure 3.9 a semicircle, centre O and radius r, is described on an isosceles right-angled triangle ABC. Segments P and Q are congruent. Find the centre of the circle which produces the segment R which is *similar* to segments P and Q.

Deduce that the area of the lune ABC is equal to the area of triangle ABC.

Mathematics schemes

In discussing the use of mathematics schemes it may be helpful to look more carefully at the demands made of teachers in preparing for whole class lessons and to compare these with the demands made when using such mathematics schemes. The structure of whole class lessons can provide the means for contrasting these different demands made of inexperienced teachers at the preparation stage.

The most obvious difference lies in the number of topics considered during a lesson. In a whole class approach the number of topics is likely to be small, a single topic being the most common case. Using a mathematics scheme with an average sized class will involve many different topics being explored simultaneously. It is important therefore to know, in the way Shulman (1986) describes knowing (see Chapter 2), what is being asked of pupils. This can only be done effectively in the first instance by noting which workcards are being used by the class and to work through these yourself. As you do this you should make notes of any difficulties you anticipate the pupils having. Such difficulties may arise from the workcards:

in the way a question is asked or in the words used to present a problem
in the way a question or problem is presented graphically
by the nature of what is being asked
by the type or quantity of resources required in order to carry out the process.

In addition, from your previous experience you may expect pupil difficulties related to:

specific content areas
reading ability
motivation
ability to concentrate.

The topic chosen for a whole class lesson will be determined by factors such as the age and ability of the class, the agreed syllabus for particular groupings, the nature of the grouping and so on. The topics 'chosen' using a mathematics scheme will be determined to a large extent by the stages at which each individual child has been demonstrated to be. This is a perceived strength of such schemes; that is, no prior judgement of abilities or pupils' previous knowledge is required on the part of the teacher. In this case there is also less chance that the teacher will predetermine the course of events and restrict the learning outcomes of a particular lesson. This is a very real danger for the inexperienced teacher adopting a whole class approach. It is also very understandable that the inexperienced teacher feels more secure the fewer outcomes there may be to a lesson. It would require a very confident student during a first teaching practice to adopt the attitude put so well by Gattegno: 'Whenever I go into a classroom to give a lesson, I am never concerned about my personal position; I am not preoccupied with my chances of success or failure or the difficulties that the particular circumstances may present' (1963:63). However, such an attitude should be one of the aims of all those aspiring to teach mathematics or any other subject. Gattegno goes on to say, almost prophetically, as it then (1956) related to whole class teaching:

I have no right to say to myself anything but: 'Each child knows what he knows, and it is thus that he will come to me. I myself shall never be able to make an inventory of his knowledge, and if the class, being an artificial group, has no common level, this is nothing but the natural result of their different lives. All I must do is to present them with a situation so elementary that they all master it from the outset, and so fertile that they will all find a great deal to get out of it. Moreover, it is possible that, liberating their energies and their perception, they will, in a few seconds, reach a point of awareness where they can survey the whole situation from afar, and even see more in it than I can myself.' (p. 63)

It is in these aspects that the sensitive use of mathematics schemes can present many, often simple but 'fertile' situations to pupils and can at the same time expose teachers in training to the needs of individual pupils, to their insights and to their enthusiasm.

As already mentioned, using a scheme such as KMP, Smile and SMP to some extent reduces the problem of choosing a topic or topics for each lesson. The requirement is that the choice is child directed and is part of an ongoing process largely determined by the structure of the scheme. Given that the topics are chosen carefully from within the concept heirarchy provided, the chances of the children being successful with the presented material is high since material has been field tested and developed over a long period and with a large number of pupils. The Kent Mathematics Project refers to this as a criterion of 80/80/80; that is 80 per cent of the teachers attained 80 per cent success in each task with 80 per cent of the children. If the criterion was met then the material would be published.

Preparing lessons using schemes

What is it then that student teachers should be concentrating upon in preparation for lessons using such schemes?

Firstly, you should try to learn as much as possible about the organization of the scheme before any attempt is made to use the scheme alone with a group of children. Even experienced teachers prefer where possible to work as a team of at least two and this may give you the opportunity to act as a support teacher to the normal class teacher. Gaining knowledge of the organization of the scheme is not, as you might think, so that you can cope with it effectively but so that you are aware of the organizational role the pupils themselves must play in minimizing the amount of administration to be done by the teachers concerned.

Action To learn where materials are kept and who might be responsible in the first instance for distribution and collection.

Secondly, since much of the teacher's time is to be spent circulating amongst individuals or groups it is essential from a confidence point of view to know something about the content and processes required by attempting the problems presented by each card or booklet. This is not so that you have immediate answers to all questions. On the contrary, you should strive to resist the temptation to show pupils a way through the problem; this merely prevents thinking on their part. What your own inside knowledge should allow you to do is to direct, stimulate and encourage through questioning all the pupils in the class whether or not they are demanding your attention. Look again in Chapter 1 at the content knowledge, pedagogical content knowledge and curricular knowledge as described by Shulman (1986).

Action To find which topics in the scheme are currently being used by the pupils, and to work through these topics at two levels: one where you bring your own mathematical skills and knowledge to bear on the problem situation; and another where you can anticipate pupil difficulties or extend pupil thinking perhaps beyond what is expected from the workcard. Clearly this exercise can form the basis of lesson preparation which can be written up in note form. Not every difficulty can be anticipated nor every question preplanned. The exercise is to raise your own awareness of the situations which should allow you to respond in a more meaningful and useful manner when required.

Thirdly, at the end of each lesson you should be in a position to know how individual pupils have progressed, the difficulties and inspirations they have had, how you should have responded to these, how you did respond and what the contingencies are for the next lesson.

Action   To include in the evaluation of the lesson the points raised above.

Fourthly, the previous point raises the whole issue of assessment and evaluation, yet another aspect of teaching you will need to come to terms with. The action suggested above should be directed largely towards your own performance using pupils' experiences, successes and failures as a mirror to aid your judgement. Part of this reflection will include some informal assessment of pupil performance through discussion. In addition to this, individual schemes require you to be systematic in marking work. This is not to say that all work should be marked by the teacher. Many schemes now readily provide answers or knowledge of results as an essential part of the move towards pupils developing a greater sense of responsibility for their own learning; pupils are encouraged to mark their own work, the teacher being responsible for checking work periodically as sets of tasks are completed. Again this can be done effectively by talking to pupils about their work as well as checking what has been written. Such schemes also provide more formal periodic testing where test books provide relevant questions about the work covered by pupils. These are handed in for the teacher to mark outside lesson time.

Action   To summarize your own role during the lesson and any points of interest and development which you ought to pursue; and to provide a summary sheet about pupil performances for your own reference.

The final task is quite crucial to the successful operation of mathematics schemes. Based on your knowledge as described by Shulman (1986) and your assessment of an individual pupil's attitude, ability and interest in the many and various topics to be covered, you have to periodically construct a new set of tasks which will form the next part of a programme of study best tailored to the needs of the particular pupil concerned. Consideration of individual successes and difficulties within topics will be pointers, but the test scores of previous tasks should be good indicators for the general level to be aimed at.

Action   Construct a new set of tasks for a pupil you know. Discuss your choice with a teacher who also has knowledge of the same pupil.

The networks provided by KMP and Smile for instance give the teacher an immediate overview of where a child is with regard to a balanced progression through the various concepts and concept levels. It should be noted that there is balance to be achieved not only across concepts but also across time so that concepts are met with fairly constant regularity. It is unlikely that progress will be the same across all concepts and you should be wary of the difficulties you may create if you force an unrealistic pace in any one direction.

It may become obvious that certain groups of children need very much the same kind of help and inspiration within a topic which only the teacher can bring about. Here is a case when your skills in talking to small groups of pupils can be exploited. There may be a need for the use of special material or apparatus or limited computer access in order to develop ideas. You may also feel that pupils should be given more opportunity to discuss strategies or findings. Identification of groups of pupils who can work together is another managerial role of the teacher which broadens the scope of mathematics schemes so that they are not strictly individualized. (It must be said that they were never intended to be so.)

Tackling teaching schemes

It would be easy to dwell too long on the detail of mathematics schemes, which are perhaps best dealt with in the teachers' guides. My aim is to give those learning to use such schemes in teaching practice some tasks which bring about a quicker understanding of the philosophy behind the implementation, and which provide the basis for a creditworthy record of events for your own reference and for those who need to assess your progress.

If you find that you are required to use a mathematics scheme for the first time:

1. Seek out the teachers who are actually using the scheme, observe what they do and talk with them about giving lessons of this type.
2. If possible show your good intentions by volunteering to help with the running of lessons prior to the practice.
3. Refer to the comprehensive teachers' guides which accompany such schemes.
4. If you get the chance, attend local or national meetings organized primarily for practising teachers to learn new skills. Your own approach and adaptability may prove very supportive.

Linking theory and practice

During the first few weeks of helping to run a mathematics scheme you should have had opportunities to develop a number of the 'distinct aspects of teaching' summarized in the Cockcroft Report paragraph 243 and discussed in Chapter 1 of this book, and perhaps to attempt to link these with the distinct aspects of learning also referred to in the Cockcroft Report: facts and skills, conceptual structures, general strategies and appreciation. However it is not at all clear, as research shows, what the nature of these links should be in relation to particular learning outcomes. Research does show that classroom interaction is dependent upon the quality of these links, and as you might imagine they are themselves dependent upon many variables associated with the teaching/learning cycle, not least the particular aspect of learning taking place and the teacher's own pedagogical content knowledge. This area is a subject of current research particularly in Britain and the United States. What follows is a discussion of a few aspects of this research which illustrate briefly the nature of such linking and how in a more general sense teacher expertise or the lack of it may affect the nature of interaction in the classroom.

A recent study (Carpenter *et al.* 1988) carried out in the United States focused on teachers' understanding of how children think mathematically and on teachers' knowledge of pupils' thinking, that is knowledge of the conceptual and procedural knowledge which pupils draw upon during the problem-solving process (in this case arithmetic problems). An important aspect of this study is the way in which it related to the ability of teachers to monitor pupils' progress in a detailed way and to use that information to decide on future teaching strategies and learning experiences; these are important aspects of any style of teaching, but particularly so if mathematics schemes are used. Before the widespread use of highly structured schemes which allow individual programmes of instruction to take place, it could be argued that one teacher keeping track of the knowledge of up to 30 pupils presented a task too demanding to contemplate. The same task using a mathematics scheme is still a daunting one but can be less so. There is a greater opportunity to raise the level and quality of knowledge about pupils' abilities. Evidence of the good intentions of mathematics schemes in this regard can be found in the KMP Teachers' Guide levels 5–9. In its discussion of spatial thinking, the necessary experiences to bring this about and the difficulties of monitoring its development, it says

It is not surprising, then, that spatial thinking, because it is difficult to analyse and describe, tends to be mentioned only in vague terms and never becomes a precise objective. It is therefore often ignored and mathematics can become a subject of symbol manipulation . . . non-cognitive aspects are difficult to analyse and define and so become obscure and often neglected. Also, like spatial thinking, these aspects can only be developed in children if we intentionally arrange experiences in which they will be developed. (p.23)

The guide goes on to elaborate how the free choice facility of the scheme allows the teacher to reach beyond what is prescribed and develop among other things the affective domain.

Carpenter *et al.* (1988) report two aspects of teacher knowledge which affect the ability to make instructional decisions: knowledge of problem difficulty, and knowledge of the strategies which pupils use to solve problems. It was found that teachers' ability to predict pupil success in solving various problems (the sort of thing you may be doing in designing another set of tasks for a pupil) correlated highly with pupil achievement on the particular problems set. However, the teachers' ability to predict the strategies that pupils would use to solve different problems was not highly correlated to pupils' problem-solving performance. This was partly due to the fact that teachers did not classify problems in terms of the strategies which pupils used to solve them; consequently it would be unlikely that this knowledge would play a major role in deciding future content and intended processes. It may be that a more sophisticated use of mathematics schemes could enhance teachers' knowledge of solution strategies, thereby improving the link between aspects of teaching and aspects of learning.

In quite separate earlier research work (Leinhardt and Smith 1985) it was found that in comparison with the inexperienced teacher, experienced teachers exhibited a more refined hierarchical structure to their knowledge when they were asked to sort a set of cards which presented fraction problems into an order representing difficulty to teach or perform. The rationale of these 'experts' was more elaborate than that of the inexperienced teacher, and the experts tended to group problems according to specific content and then by problem difficulty, whereas the novice had fewer groupings and was not aware of much differentiation in problem difficulty. The same research revealed that in presenting lessons on fractions there was much 'disparity between the teachers' ability to express an algorithm and their lack of understanding of the underlying mathematical concepts and relationships'. This may well reflect the teachers' learning of fractions at an early stage which has for many years been taught as a topic requiring only skill acquisition. The National Curriculum defines attainment targets in terms of knowledge, skills and understanding, and although there is some detail about what this means with regard to content there is little here for the novice in trying to come to terms with the complexities of teaching for understanding. For example attainment target 3 (DES 1989: 9–11), which covers fractions among other things, is expressed almost entirely in terms of what the pupils are expected to be able to do. Although 'understanding' is in the heading for this target, little regard is paid to it in the detail. Words such as 'solve', 'calculate', 'work out', 'convert', 'use' exemplify how much emphasis, intended or not, is placed on procedures. There is little evidence of any attempt to obtain a balance between procedural and conceptual development.

It is important for the mathematics teacher to know as much as possible pupils' patterns of thinking; that is, the emphasis should be on what the pupil thinks rather than what he/she does. It is not difficult to see why the latter predominates. Activity, purposeful or not, has been seen either as a way forward or as a way in which an overstretched teacher can gain some breathing space in coping with a large class.

If we are to embrace the constructivists' theory that action is a precondition for learning then we must concentrate our efforts into improving the nature of classroom activity. It is not sufficient to rely solely on the procedural aspects of 'acquiring knowledge' in the vain hope that some glimmer of understanding will emerge. Research shows that the link between doing and understanding is a tenuous one, unique to the individual (Hiebert and Wearne 1986). Teaching strategies which, by design or default, cause a rift or separation between doing and understanding, by promoting only a superficial activity by pupils, encouraged in the past by syllabus and examination demands, can lead to damaging failures. 'The instructional problem is to design experiences in which skill and understanding will both be acquired in an integrated fashion' (Greeno 1985:239).

Before putting forward some general guidelines it may be useful to look more closely at Hiebert and Wearne's (1986) definitions of conceptual and procedural knowledge and to try to relate these to pupils' experiences whilst trying to solve problems. Conceptual knowledge they define as 'knowledge of those facts and properties of mathematics that are recognized as being related in some way . . . [it] is distinguished primarily by the relationships between pieces of information' (p. 200). Procedural knowledge on the other hand is about rules not relationships; the rules govern the manipulation of symbols and determine the order in which things are to be done. The authors also identify three important stages in the problem-solving process where the linking of skills and understanding can be crucial:

interpreting the problem
selecting and applying procedures
checking the reasonableness of solutions

They illustrate the importance of the linking of skills and understanding at the first point by using a fraction example: $7/8 \div 1/4$. A correct beginning to the solution would result from drawing upon two quite different areas of knowledge: firstly, the symbol 'divide' may evoke the procedure 'invert the second fraction and multiply'; but secondly, relating the symbol 'divide' to the asking of the question 'How many quarters are there in seven-eighths?' demonstrates that some reference to a conceptual framework is being made.

The second stage of the problem-solving process is to apply the chosen procedure. It is precisely this area which in the past has been given a disproportionate amount of time in the mathematics curriculum. Much of the responsibility placed on pupils has been in the form of correctly remembering a set of rules or imitating a given procedure and there has been little demand for pupils (and in some cases teachers) to link skills with understanding. It is clear that the ability to refer to some conceptual knowledge base at the first stage forms an important basis on which any inductive argument can be developed which makes sense of the rule 'invert and multiply'.

The final stage in the process is to check on the reasonableness of the answer. If applied correctly, practised skills will give the correct result, but they can in no way contribute to the judgement about reasonableness. Although it could be argued that reference to any conceptual framework alone could not be expected to yield the result $3\frac{1}{2}$ exactly, the presence of a conceptualization of fraction knowledge should lead the solver to the conclusion that the answer ought to be a little less than 4. What follows are two examples of how such external referents can be used to check on reasonableness. This may occur from a variety of linkages or routes; some may give a rough guide, others may give an answer as accurate as that produced by skilfully applying a correct procedure. For example, $\frac{7}{8}$ is slightly less than 1; 1 divided by $\frac{1}{4}$ means 'How many quarters in one whole?', answer 4; so $\frac{7}{8}$ divided by $\frac{1}{4}$ is somewhat less than 4. Another form of plausible reasoning may take the following form: $\frac{7}{8}$ divided by $\frac{1}{8}$ means 'How many eighths in seven-eighths?', answer 7; since $\frac{1}{4}$ is twice $\frac{1}{8}$, the answer to the original question is half of 7, that is $3\frac{1}{2}$.

It can be argued that the ability to draw upon both these aspects of knowledge near simultaneously at each stage of the problem-solving process demonstrates that mastery has been achieved. However, it is not advocated that each time a problem is solved both processes should be applied at each stage of solution; this would be a waste of mental energy. Again it appears to be a question of balance in applying the right kind of mathematical thinking to bring about desired learning outcomes at the right time. It is a question of much debate just how much content should be routinized and to what extent it should be pursued. It is generally agreed that initially activities should be directed towards understanding, with links to the concrete, rather than towards wholesale early replacement of activities by symbolic manipulation or the construction of a symbol system which can become an independent entity for those who are able to cope with the necessary abstractions which go with it (Hiebert 1988). Decisions about this are affected not least by the introduction of new technologies into the mathematics curriculum which serve to reduce the need to recall facts and remember routines. From the teacher's and the educationalist's point of view there are three important questions to answer in order to improve our understanding of the learning process (Hiebert and Wearne 1986):

1. How is conceptual knowledge formed?
2. How do mathematical symbols become viewed as representations of conceptual content?

3. How do algorithms become viewed as prescriptions for carrying out with symbols what are meaningful operations on conceptual content?

It seems then that the implications for mathematics teaching, put succinctly by Grouws (1988) are: 'What is needed is instruction that focuses on development and the meaning of ideas, with a goal of achieving diversity of student thought and the use of a variety of solution methods and techniques' (p. 6).

There is a great risk in oversimplifying the situation when one comes to giving practical advice, but this may be a necessary step in order that research findings become a tool which the teacher can use to develop a personal kind of pedagogy. So from a practical point of view, inexperienced teachers should be on their guard against designing lessons which aim to develop skills strictly through repetitive practice which may have no meaning or to encourage pupils to apply another person's algorithms without giving thought to why they might work. Generally lessons which are designed to give pupils time to think and reflect are rare, yet thinking and reflecting are at the heart of doing mathematics. If we see *doing* mathematics as a prerequisite to understanding new concepts then we have to encourage children to think about what they are doing, and if we wish to develop the application of mathematics then we have to encourage children to think about what it is they are about to do and the contexts in which the mathematics applies.

Suggested exercise

Develop a scheme of work for a known group of children or design a new matrix of tasks for a pupil you know. Take into consideration the following points:

1. Try to bring together topics which are related in some way. Aim at building a wholeness using a general theme or themes.
2. Develop concepts in a systematic way, building on previously learned skills and ideas. The network structure of the mathematics schemes discussed in this chapter allows for this to happen in a natural way. Do not forget to add your own contribution and interpretation where you think fit.
3. There will be plenty of scope to develop your own ideas about how the mathematics presented in books or through schemes might relate to real life.
4. Try to keep a balance between topics requiring individual study and those which require working with and discussing with others.
5. Operationally try to keep a watchful eye for different pupil

approaches for solving problems and be prepared to discuss them. Do not be tempted to impose your own algorithms as a quick solution to overcome an early impasse which pupils may experience.

This chapter has sought to draw your attention to the differences and similarities between providing your own framework for lessons or using published schemes of work. It has emphasized the importance, from a personal development point of view, of making your own contribution to lesson preparation regardless of the method chosen. A brief discussion of some of the related theoretical ideas has attempted to give you some background against which some reflection and generation of new ideas may take place. The next chapter considers in more detail those factors regarded as having a significant influence on the quality of the learning process.

Further reading

Ahmed A. 1987 *Better Mathematics: a Curriculum Development Study* HMSO, Chapters 2 and 6

CHAPTER 4

Enriching the process of learning

The previous chapter attempted to outline some of the various approaches for teaching and learning now available to the mathematics teacher. No combination of approaches can guarantee success with each and every pupil for each and every teacher. It is hoped that the points raised there will help the inexperienced teacher to form a sound base on which to build in preparing for and giving interesting lessons. Reaching the stage where one can feel reasonably confident about preparing and managing a successful lesson is no simple task and demands more than a modicum of energy, thoughtfulness and skill to develop. Anyone who does not think so is underestimating the complex nature of teaching well.

But what are the factors which distinguish lessons that are competently given from those that encourage pupils to think mathematically, change attitudes or even inspire? The answers to this question are quite elusive. Even knowing the answers cannot ensure that a lesson will meet its targets. We can, as a start, begin to learn to avoid the mathematically harmful processes which are so easily administered. An amusing but chillingly true comparison between 'junk food' and 'junk mathematics' is given in Ahmed (1987: 15).

If we accept the suggestion that natural curiosity drives inventiveness and that the child's natural curiosity declines after the age of 7 (Desforges and Cockburn 1987:5) then our task as secondary teachers of mathematics is a daunting one. Those seeking to sustain lessons which not only meet their targets in terms of content learned but also attempt to set and meet process targets through a richness of activity will above all require patience with themselves over time in order to reach a level of experience which allows a glimpse of what might be achieved under ideal conditions. Inevitably giving lessons which seek to be different in the way in which children are challenged carries different risks, and many would say in particular a greater risk of falling short of what is intended. It may be that we should not or indeed cannot over-prescribe our objectives for these kinds of lessons. If we are to provide mathematics which nourishes rather than the 'junk mathematics' referred to above, then the risks have to be taken. In truth there seems little to be lost by adopting a more enterprising approach which seeks to develop enquiring minds through enjoyable purposeful activity. Knowledge of and the ability to develop fertile but simple situations for children to explore is at the heart of this approach. *Knowledge of* a problem or situation does not necessarily mean *knowledge about* it, and much can be gained by genuinely exploring new ground together.

Enrichment processes based on curriculum models are well documented. Many of these accounts will be found in books dedicated to the education of the gifted or talented pupil. It is the intention of this chapter not to dwell exclusively on the gifted pupil but to try to determine which factors considered important for enriching the process of learning for the gifted pupil can be reasonably taken account of by student teachers in developing their teaching skills with all pupils. A discussion of some well known general theories as they relate to the cognitive and affective domains across all subjects and how they might manifest themselves in the mathematics classroom may be of practical benefit in providing more challenging mathematics lessons.

There is sufficient consistency in the principles expounded by the theories for enrichment of learning for me to mention just two. Bloom's (1956) taxonomy of cognitive development is perhaps the best known classification of the learning process and is based, as the word 'taxonomy' indicates, on a single principle or a consistent set of principles. In Bloom's case a *principle of complexity* reflected the order of difficulty of the learning of different objectives, and appeared at a time when much interest was being shown in objectives and how they influenced teaching and learning. Later work on the affective domain (Krathwohl *et al.* 1964) proved more difficult to structure and received less acclaim. The classification of cognitive activity could be used by teachers to develop their teaching from a position of imparting knowledge and facilitating understanding to one of providing more challenging activities such as analysing relationships, determining patterns, creating patterns, suggesting methods to a solution and comparing their effectiveness or consistency. The cognitive domain is classified as follows:

knowledge
comprehension
application
analysis
synthesis
evaluation.

For a concise version of Bloom's taxonomy which describes subclasses within these six main levels, see Krathwohl *et al.* (1964: Appendix B).

It has been suggested that a good model for teaching the gifted could be based on an inverted pyramid shape which gives more curriculum time to the more difficult areas of applications, analysis and synthesis, and that for average pupils more time should be spent acquiring and demonstrating basic skills. This may be sound advice, but curriculum planning for the average and even less able should not exclude opportunities which encourage a more independent approach through which basic skills and higher-level thinking skills become integrated and task oriented. The National Curriculum, which lays down more specific guidelines for teaching with an emphasis on knowledge, skills and understanding (at the lower end of Bloom's taxonomy) and the linking of this with national testing at 7, 11, and 14, is likely to have an adverse effect on teacher directed enrichment processes, even though 'programmes of study were to be broad enough to leave scope for teachers to use their professional talents and skills to develop schemes of work' (DES 1988: paragraph 4.13).

The second curriculum model, the Williams (1970) model, is included because it was designed not specifically for teaching gifted pupils but for teaching all pupils. The model as shown in Figure 4.1 covers along dimension 1 the subject matter for a number of subjects. If we were to adopt the model for a mathematics programme then each subject could be replaced by an area within the mathematics curriculum, for example number, algebra, measures, shape and space, and data handling as classified in the national curriculum proposals for mathematics (DES 1988). Dimension 2 in the Williams model lists 18 activities and skills which teachers can employ in determining the pupil behaviours given along dimension 3. Most of the 18 activities have a direct relevance to the teaching of mathematics and have been broadly classified under three types of activity: exploration, training and production (Renzulli 1977:14). The first two types of activity (being exploration and training), that is purposeful activity with a minimum of imposed structure, and processes concerned with dealing more effectively with content, are considered appropriate teaching approaches for all children.

Clearly there are a number of factors which appear to contribute to enrichment of content, of learning processes and of teaching strategies, all of which relate to the education of the gifted pupil and many of which can be beneficially employed in learning situations for the majority of pupils.

Some of the foregoing discussion may seem like overkill for student teachers seeking to improve their mathematics teaching. Natural questions would seem to be: what can be learnt from these models? How can such knowledge be applied to enrich classroom processes? A good strategy may be to choose one or two aspects which lie within each dimension on the Williams model which you can immediately identify with and to concentrate on these.

In general terms then the first requirement appears to be that of finding appropriate situations which motivate and which can be

Figure 4.1 Model for Implementing Cognitive-Affective Behaviours in the Classroom (Williams 1970)

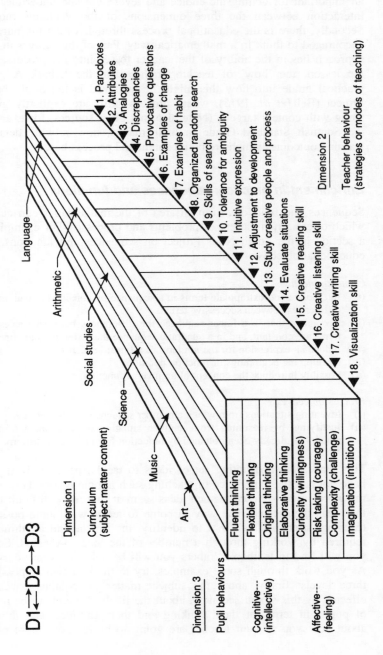

explored at the right level. The teacher's judgement about pupils' behaviour, affective as well as cognitive, under given circumstances is all important for getting the choice and level right and underlines the interaction between the three dimensions of the Williams model. Secondly, there is the educational process through which the pupil is encouraged to think in a mathematical way. Part of the success in this approach lies in the ability of the teacher to see into the processes of the lesson, the 'how' of teaching rather than the 'what'. A good practical guide into how this might be achieved is the South Notts Project (Bell *et al.* 1975), where process skills are explicitly given along with content targets. (Note also that other sources, for example the Scottish Standard Grade in mathematics, now provide detailed learning outcomes which are both content and process based.)

Enrichment in practice: sequences and functions

Sequences and functions form an area of the mathematics curriculum which offers a rich variety of problems and processes. For example in a section in the South Notts Project on sequences and functions, the educational objectives read:

Content objectives
(i)   Interpolate and extrapolate terms in a sequence by considering patterns of differences between successive terms.
(ii) Recognize that in a linear sequence the differences between successive terms are constant, and in a quadratic sequence the differences are linear.
(iii) Induce an expression for the nth term of a linear sequence.
(iv) Develop the beginnings of function notation.
(v)   Possibly introduce the concept of an inverse function.

Process objectives
(i)   Inventing situations from which a number sequence can be derived.
(ii) Justifying, by reasoning from a given situation or diagram, a formula which has already been obtained by induction from a number pattern.

This may seem a daunting set of ideas to tackle, particularly if you have not had the experience of teaching such a topic before. However, the words used to describe such ideas seem at first more difficult than the ideas themselves. The way to come to terms with some possible teaching strategies is first to identify the mathematical thinking required by working through a number of the ideas presented. Some you will find in textbooks, others you will be able to invent yourself. As you work through some examples, try to think at two or possibly three levels: firstly, about the subject matter or syllabus coverage effected by this study; secondly, about the likely demands to be made of pupils in terms of their thinking and their attitudes; and thirdly, about how you as their teacher are going to bring about these pupil behaviours. A few examples and some discussion follow. The ideas are not constrained by the time available in either a lesson or a series of lessons, and you will have to determine what is possible under any given set of circumstances.

A number of processes can be identified, their richness deriving from an underlying theme of patterns. Patterns can be analysed, hypotheses put forward verbally, informally or more formally in terms of a formula representing a generalization. The reverse process may take place, working backwards to verify the generalization. (Note that the word 'proof' does not appear in any of this work.) The processes are as follows:

1. Identifying a pattern by determining missing terms in a sequence, or by continuing a sequence.
2. Moving from number patterns to rules.
3. Moving from rules to number patterns.
4. Moving from diagrams to number patterns and then to rules.
5. Moving from rules to number patterns and then to diagrams.
6. Generating patterns, identifying rules.
7. Inventing rules, generating patterns.

An example of each follows.

Identifying patterns in sequences

(a) Fill in the blanks so that your answers complete the following pattern:

  15,   31,   63,   *,   *,   511

(b) Write down the next two terms in the following sequence:

  0.5,   0.75,   1.0,   1.25,   1.5,   *,   *

Moving from number patterns to rules

Note that if the process in (a) and (b) above is to obtain the missing numbers by finding a rule which connects consecutive terms in the sequence, then the order of difficulty is roughly the same. A rule to generate the first sequence is 'multiply by 2 and add 1', and one for the second sequence is 'add one-quarter'. However, identifying a rule for the nth term in each of these sequences is not roughly of equal difficulty. Constant first differences of one-quarter in the second sequence imply that the nth term will be of the form $(1/4)n \pm$ constant. For the first sequence the first and successive differences increase by a factor of two, implying that the nth term will be exponential in form; such notions are beyond many following a mainstream mathematics course.

Moving from rules to number patterns

Write down three different number sequences which obey the rule 'each term is the sum of the two preceding ones'.

Here again the problem is left as open as possible; only the rule for generation is specified. So sequences as seemingly diverse as

2, 5, 7, 12, 19, 31, . . .

0, 1, 1, 2, 3, 5, . . .

−2, −4, −6, −10, −16, . . .

have a sameness about the way they are generated. Seeking a general expression for the nth term in these cases is not a trivial activity, but enrichment can nevertheless be pursued by suggesting that any pair or indeed all three of the above sequences might be added together. Does the rule still apply? Alternatively each sequence might be multiplied by a constant and the same question asked. Changing one word in the original rule, i.e. from 'sum' to 'difference', opens up the activity dramatically.

Moving from diagrams to number patterns to rules

Common examples under this category are the number patterns formed by using spatial arrangements of shapes (NCAT 5 levels 1–7), such as the following:

Figure 4.2 **Triangular numbers**

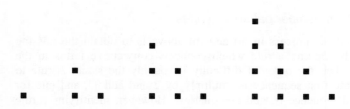

Triangular (Figure 4.2):   1,   3,   6,   10,   . . .

Figure 4.3 **Square numbers**

Square (Figure 4.3): 1, 4, 9, 16, . . .

Figure 4.4 **Pentagonal numbers**

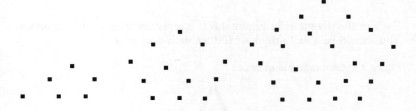

Pentagonal (Figure 4.4): 1, 5, 12, 22, . . .

Figure 4.5 **Hexagonal numbers**

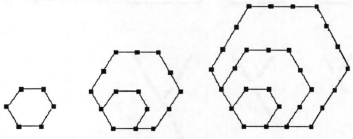

Hexagonal (Figure 4.5): 1, 6, 15, 28, . . .

These sequences have respectively constant second differences (i.e. the difference between consecutive first differences) of 1, 2, 3 and 4, indicating that the general term for each will be quadratic. Further inspection reveals the following expressions for the nth terms:

Triangular: $(n^2 + n)/2$
Square: n^2
Pentagonal: $(3n^2 - n)/2$
Hexagonal: $(4n^2 - 2n)/2$

Changing the format for square numbers to $(2n^2 - 0n)/2$ reveals a pattern within a pattern which leads to the conjecture that the nth term of a sequence of p-gonal numbers is $\{(p - 2)n^2 - (p - 4)n\}/2$.

Moving from rules to number patterns to diagrams

This activity can encourage originality. Its openness lies in the freedom it offers for pupils to invent diagrams which illustrate a number sequence. Even simple sequences can lead to interesting patterns. For example, the rule $n \rightarrow 3n$ generates the table

1, 2, 3, 4, 5, . . .

3, 6, 9, 12, 15, . . .

Each of the diagrams in Figure 4.6 is a representation of the sequence. You should be able to think of further such diagrams.

Figure 4.6 **Generating sequences**

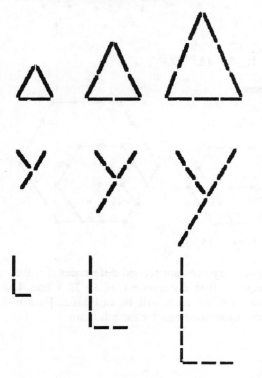

Generating patterns, identifying rules

*Figure 4.7 **Sequence for completion***

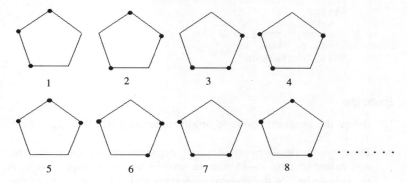

Draw the next two diagrams in the sequence, given in Figure 4.7.

In this case a geometric pattern is generated by a rule applied to each set of dots in turn. Identifying a rule is identifying a sameness which exists between each diagram and its immediate neighbours. This example illustrates how a problem situation can be *open*. The openness lies in not imposing ideas about how the dots may move. Labelling the dots in any way would close down the situation at this initial exploratory stage.

The reader is invited to determine at least two simple rules for generating the sequence. Determining the *n*th term in such a sequence has little meaning. Possible links between consecutive or alternate 'terms' and if or when the sequence repeats itself are more rewarding questions to be asked.

Inventing rules, generating patterns

This can be fun as well as instructive. Complicated sequences can soon be generated from a simple rule or rules. For example,

$$n \rightarrow \begin{cases} n^2/4 & \text{for } n \text{ even} \\ (n^2 - 1)/4 & \text{for } n \text{ odd} \end{cases}$$

generates the following sequence for $n = 1, \ 2, \ 3, \ . \ . \ . :$

$$0, \ 1, \ 2, \ 4, \ 6, \ 9, \ 12, \ 16, \ 20, \ . \ . \ .$$

For those familiar with BBC Basic, the following short program taken from Higgo *et al.* (1985) takes the drudgery out of producing a sequence from a given rule:

```
10   PRINT'' Enter formula for nth term in terms of n''
20   INPUT £$
30   n=1
40   PRINT''n'';TAB(5);''Term''
50   REPEAT
60     t=EVAL(f$)
70     PRINT;n;TAB(5);t
80     n=n+1
90   UNTIL FALSE:END
```

Exercise

1. Adapt the program above to produce the sequence 0, 1, 2, 4, 6, 9, 12, 16, 20, . . .

2. Describe in detail possible pupil experiences sufficient for the equivalent of two 35–45 minute lessons which attempt to realize (a) at least one of the content objectives and (b) at least one of the process objectives listed earlier from the South Notts Project for sequences and functions. Say how you would attempt to assess whether your objectives had been achieved.

3. (a) A slot machine will take only 1p or 2p. Investigate the number of possible arrangements of coins used to make payment of various amounts. For example, to pay 4p one may use one of five possible arrangements:

   1p, 1p, 1p, 1p;   1p, 1p, 2p;   1p, 2p, 1p;   2p, 1p, 1p;   2p, 2p

   Examine the sequence for pattern, try to justify the form of the sequence, and make some generalizations.

   (b) Using a pinboard and elastic bands, form a number of different straight-edged plane figures (concave as well as convex) and complete a table with the following column headings:

   number of pins on perimeter (p) (points with integer coordinates)
   number of pins inside (q) (points with integer coordinates)
   area in unit squares (A)

   (Alternatively, draw the figures on squared paper.)
   Find a relation connecting A, p and q. Devise a series of graduated steps and questions which would lead a child of 12 to discover this relation.

Part of the success of the enrichment process, not yet discussed, lies at the teacher strategy level. One instance of this is the teacher's ability at some stage of a problem-solving situation to retreat from the front line of attack, otherwise there is a great risk that the teacher's solution will emerge rather than the pupil's solution. Retreating from the problem situation does not of course mean a wholesale withdrawal of interest; retreating in this sense means listening well, giving help only when judged to be needed, assessing the validity of arguments without necessarily responding, and being open-minded about new lines of development. All this very much depends upon the teacher's ability to judge how much knowledge pupils may have to draw on and how they will persevere with a problem – an interaction between dimension 2 and dimension 3 of the Williams model. There is always an element of risk in pursuing approaches which facilitate more independent thinking by pupils; the largest risk is that pupils will lose interest or concentration because of lack of progress, particularly if this is a relatively new experience for them. If this happens with a number of pupils then the teacher's general management skills will be an important factor in maintaining lesson momentum. Instances of teachers maintaining momentum, largely through skilful interaction during the problem-solving phase, without overdirecting events are reported in the journals *Mathematics Teaching* (Association of Teachers of Mathematics) and *Mathematics in Schools* (Mathematical Association).

The few ideas presented here as a move towards preparing and presenting richer lessons are not new and will be revisited and discussed more fully in Chapter 6 in the context of problem solving and investigative work. The main purpose of this chapter is to explore some of the possible sources of enrichment for teaching and learning. This enrichment appears to have its sources in the nature of the content, the processes by which content is covered, and how each of these factors may, if at all, influence the other. The act of bringing together these sources of enrichment is laid squarely on the teacher and what he/she can provide within the classroom environment. The fact that many classrooms lend themselves to formal chalk and talk methods and little else makes the task even more of an uphill struggle: 'Classrooms as presently conceived and resourced are simply not good places in which to expect the development of the sorts of higher order skills currently desired from a mathematics curriculum' (Desforges and Cockburn 1987:139). This statement is made within the context of the primary mathematics curriculum, but my observations of many secondary mathematics classrooms leaves me in no doubt that the sentiments conveyed are equally pertinent to the way in which the secondary mathematics curriculum is 'conceived and resourced'. The secondary mathematics classroom consisting of four or five rows of double desks all facing an overused chalkboard with little else in evidence is still the norm rather than the exception.

It is easy to blame teachers for this state of affairs, but it would be wrong to lay the whole blame here. There are many pressures working against change: not the least is that measurable targets can still be reached by changing little, and new targets which are not easily measurable and which demand different approaches are adjusted slightly to make them more accessible, or remain very much in the background (see Desforges and Cockburn (1987) for a fuller discussion).

Computers and their effects upon the teaching of mathematics

There is no single instructional aid which can assume anything like the potential of the computer in the task of enriching the processes of learning mathematics. The potential lies in the computer's power and versatility to enhance whatever is known to exist as content and to create new areas of interest and application; potential lies also in the way mathematical activity can be extended in both range and depth. 'Computers shape and enhance the power of mathematics, while mathematics shapes and enhances the power of computers. Each forces the other to grow and change, creating, in Thomas Kuhn's language, a new mathematical paradigm' (Steen 1986: 52). It is for these succinctly expressed reasons that part of this chapter is devoted to the uses of computers in mathematics teaching in the secondary school.

Most readers will be familiar with much of the existing content of secondary school mathematics and will relate to this content through their own learning experiences. It is likely except in a minority of cases that these experiences are rooted in the traditional learning environment discussed in earlier chapters. A useful starting point in using computers in the mathematics classroom may be to recognize and select familiar topics which can be approached experimentally. The use of a computer in this experimentation will of course depend either upon existing software and its quality or upon the user's programming skills. Mathematically oriented software is now more available and, since many attempts at direct instruction have been suspended, much of the software recently written lends itself readily to exploratory use. Already the 'forcing' referred to by Steen becomes apparent. If the teacher is to use this kind of software and explore the full effects both as an electronic blackboard and as a learning aid in an investigatory mode, then changes in presentation and process will have to be made. Used in an exploratory way the situation immediately gives control of the learning environment to the pupil, active learning is encouraged and the pupil begins to think and discover for himself.

Many mathematically rich situations can be presented where the software need not support sophisticated interaction. It may be for example that all that is required is for diagrams to be presented quickly and accurately, allowing the user to change at will one or more features in order to move from a number of special cases to a more generalized statement; this is an important link between experimental activity and the more formal aspects of mathematics. (One or two examples can be found in Chapter 6.)

The same software can often be used in at least two ways to support learning within a lesson: firstly in an exploratory way by the pupil or small group, and then by the teacher in attempting to bring together and extend ideas on a whole class basis. A situation to guard against, as before, is that of presenting pupils with problems which are mathematically too demanding and require too much teacher direction in the early stages. If this is avoided, the topic should become enriched through the pupil's own activity, the enrichment being seated in the pupil's abilities and curiosity.

Almost all the current content of the secondary school syllabus can be covered in this way. I am not advocating that it should be exclusively so but there is little evidence to suggest that the thoughtful use of computers as an instructional aid is harmful in any area of the mathematics curriculum. The least positive account found (Clark 1983:445) of the effects of media on learning indicates that claims of enhancement of performance and time gains are vulnerable to 'rival hypotheses' (p. 448) such as uncontrolled effects of novelty and changes in instructional method; yet in summary it is conceded that computers are 'delivery vehicles for instruction and do not directly influence learning' (p. 453).

Another meta-analysis of the effect of computer-based teaching was undertaken by Kulik, *et al.* (1983). Database searches revealed 51 such studies which contained findings in six major areas: exam performance, retention, attitudes towards content, attitudes towards instruction, attitudes towards computers, and time to learn. Significant gains were found in all six areas. A recent study of the wider use of instructional aids in mathematics teaching (Raphael and Wahlstrom 1989) looked at three areas of the curriculum: geometry; ratio, proportion and percentage; and measurement. In the first two it was found that the use of instructional aids contributed to greater content coverage which in turn led to greater pupil achievement. Only in the teaching of measurement was the use of instructional aids found to be unrelated to pupil achievement. The research also found that use of teaching aids varied according to the experience of the teachers: the more experienced the teacher the greater the use, although occasional use in geometry had a more beneficial effect than extensive use. Recent research also indicates that the use of different types of computer software can bring about significant changes in the social behaviours of children during problem-solving activity (see Chapter 7 on Logo and mathematics).

Clearly the business of enriching the process of learning is a complex one. Many factors, including epistemological ones, influence the quality of the outcome. The purpose of this chapter is not to pursue these factors in depth, but simply to point out a number of ways in which enrichment can happen and encourage readers to experiment.

The content of the mathematics curriculum has been in times past divided into the three areas of geometry, number and algebra. This was done partly in order to facilitate the teaching of concepts within any one area. They were perceived to be sufficiently unconnected with concepts in other areas to enable little conflict to arise in the sequencing of work. Reports official and otherwise have also found it convenient to divide the content into distinct areas; the most recent are those put forward in the national curriculum (DES 1989), where the five areas of number, algebra, measures, space and shape, and handling data are listed. It is indicative of the changes that have taken place in how we perceive the mathematics curriculum that these five areas are dealt with as overlapping. For example, the development of number into number patterns and sequences leads naturally into symbolic notation which represents the generalized situation (see for example NCAT5, where number targets and algebra targets run together). Much overlap is readily identified across all three of the traditional areas. These common areas have developed through the efforts of teachers and educationalists over the years to bring together in a more cohesive way the various branches of mathematics. Many links have developed not through an explicit attempt to create them but through attempts at enriching the learning process. Where this has been done successfully it has led to an opening-up process which allows various mathematical ideas to come together in one exploration. Potential uses of the computer in this regard are being identified and its influence on the mathematics curriculum is just beginning to be realized.

The following sections illustrate the computer's potential for mathematics teaching.

Handling both numeric and non-numeric data

The power in handling numeric data is most forcibly demonstrated by the use of spreadsheets. The power is derived from a number of attributes. A spreadsheet is context free so that applications can be wide ranging. The rules governing the manipulation of data are constant and easily learned. Only the content of cells and their interrelationships determine the character of a spreadsheet. They allow problem solving and investigatory modes of working (Simmons 1990). They also allow different levels of working by pupils, from entering data into a teacher prepared template to designing and programming a spreadsheet to solve their own problems.

The ability to use non-numeric data is widening as technologies develop. The selection of options using icon menus and a mouse driven pointer is becoming a standard way of building and executing computer screen models. Two relatively recent pieces of software for the Archimedes microcomputer which illustrate these properties are Numerator from Logotron and Mouse Plotter from the Shell Centre, Nottingham (aspects of Numerator are described briefly below).

Developing logical thinking through computer programming

There is a special relationship between computer programming and solving mathematical problems, historically and operationally. Being able to program in a language such as Basic or learning the language of a spreadsheet allows ideas to be explored in a dynamic way in a different medium. For example the recurrence relation $u_{n+1} = u_n + u_{n-1}$ with u_0 and u_1 defined may be all encompassing for the experienced mathematician but is much less so for those unfamiliar with such relations. The facility to build this into a small computer program or to represent it as a series of interconnected modules as in Numerator changes the nature of the relation from one that is apparently static to one that is dynamic and has pattern. The fact that Basic for instance has limitations from a purist programming point of view really does not matter. What is important is that pupils have other ways of expressing their mathematical thinking, can see the results of such thinking and where necessary can make adjustments to both procedures and concepts. Figures 4.8 and 4.9 illustrate how relatively simple it is to dynamically represent the above recurrence relation with $u_0 = 1$ and $u_1 = 2$ using Numerator in terms of 'number tanks' and 'processors' and to produce a graph which shows that the ratio of consecutive terms as the process continues tends to a limit and how the limit is reached.

Figure 4.8 **Representation of recurrence process**

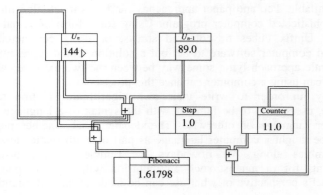

Figure 4.9 **Result of recurrence process**

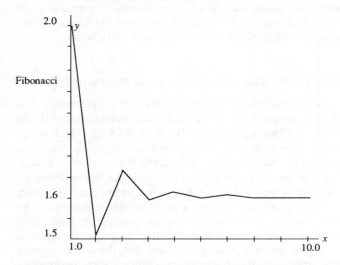

This assumes a computer culture which is still absent from many mathematics classrooms. 'You know that you have really grasped a mathematical process if you can program a machine to perform it. This implies a teaching style which, at the moment, is hardly to be found' (Fletcher 1983:18). Some purist mathematicians would argue the validity of the first statement. I believe that no one can argue that the second is not as true today as it was in 1983.

Increased availability of the algorithmic approach to problem solving

An algorithmic approach to solving problems has always been an option open to pupils and teachers whether or not computers have been available. Pen and paper approaches can be as much algorithmic as a sophisticated computer program. Using some form of visual aid such as Unifix cubes or coloured straws, or using commercially produced computer software to act out a solution, could represent an algorithmic approach lying some way between the two extreme cases. So how can using a computer enhance this process?

Firstly, in order to write their own algorithmic solution to a problem, users need to be familiar with the syntax of a language – a computer language or otherwise. The debate about whether pupils should be taught a computer language as part of mathematics lessons still rumbles along, but nowadays the rumble is very distant. Arguments for or against such an inclusion will depend upon an individual's perspective of what use can be made of an understanding of a computer language. Those who feel strongly that there is practical value in having such knowledge will no doubt find the energy and time to invest in its teaching. An overcrowded mathematics curriculum will prevent those teachers who feel less strongly about programming potential from doing anything about it. In order to move from a situation where just a few enthusiasts teach and use a mathematical programming language to a situation where programming computers is seen as another way of channelling mathematical thinking which has validity as well as practicality, fundamental questions still need to be addressed about the nature of mathematical education in our schools. The kinds of programming skills I am arguing for here are not the skills required for producing widely used packages, but those skills which allow the birth of a mathematical idea to take place through the medium of a computer language. Programs of this nature are characterized by many of the short programs to be found in Higgo *et al.* (1985). Writing even a six-line program, as the introduction to the book says, 'requires a careful analysis of the topic, and . . . running the program provides for greater insight into what is going on' (p. 5). The opening line giving advice to 'throw the book away' (when it has been read) indicates the authors' strength of feeling about the ability which pupils (and teachers) ought to have in order to write their own programs. Again it does not really matter if the language used is Basic as long as ideas can be expressed by using it. It is no good expounding the virtues of say Prolog and at the same time criticizing the inadequacies of Basic if Basic and its variants can be used to good effect to learn mathematics whereas, because of difficulties in learning the language, Prolog cannot.

Improved social and cognitive interactions between pupils

The fears expressed about the dangers of pupil isolation in the early days of using computers in educational settings are now dispelled. These fears are beginning to be replaced by a cautious optimism that the thoughtful use of computers can bring about a number of desired changes in the learning environment. Whether working with a computer language or using a commercially produced learning package, pupils who work together in pairs exploring situations created by their own efforts (e.g. programming in Logo) or exploring situations created by others (e.g. Shell Centre/JMB 'Pirates') appear to be less inhibited about putting forward their ideas, initially through discussion. This may be because the computer can act as a final arbiter in coming to the right decisions about possible moves in seeking a solution. What seems to be an important spin-off from this close cooperative work at the computer keyboard is that pupils are prepared to work in a similar fashion away from the computer, returning to have ideas verified. Other factors which appear to be enhanced are persistence after encountering a difficulty, the ability through collaboration to determine what is required and the pleasure shown when success is achieved.

A cognitive technology is defined as 'any medium that helps transcend the limitations of the mind in thinking, learning, and problem solving activities' (Pea 1987:91). Pea goes on to describe two types of function in cognitive technology as it is applied to the learning of mathematics; the functions transcend the mathematics being learned. The types are *purpose* functions and *process* functions; the former are concerned with affecting whether or not the pupil wants to think mathematically, the latter with supporting mathematical thinking once it has begun. Purpose functions are 'ownership', 'self-worth' and 'knowledge for action'. The theory suggests that ownership of ideas in this context is more easily come by; that self-worth comes about through encouraging an 'incremental view of intelligence' which brings about understanding through a willingness to test ideas; and that knowledge for action allows for the solution of real world problems and enhances contextual relevance.

Process functions support mathematical thinking by developing 'conceptual fluency', allowing 'mathematical exploration', supporting the integration of 'different mathematical representations', 'learning how to learn' and 'learning problem-solving methods' (Pea 1987:106). Pea suggests that these are clearly identified in mathematics education. Below is my attempt at identifying some computer activities more familiar to the British scene. Identification is not difficult; what becomes obvious is that few processes fall into only one of these categories.

Conceptual fluency is enhanced by freeing the user from routine tasks which are secondary to the main problem area. For example, at one level this may be superimposing the graphs of two functions to compare y values over a certain range; the chore of plotting is removed, and energies can be directed towards the properties of the two graphs. At another level a less able child can find new ways of thinking about say the size of fractions, having been freed temporarily from a purely symbolic way of expressing them.

Mathematical exploration within a computer environment may start through the ability to ask 'what happens if' questions. The facility to see the results of an idea almost immediately is both exciting and worrying. What worries educationalists about this instant feedback is that it can work against mathematical thinking, that exploration within a computer environment may remain at a superficial level without any conjecture being made and subsequently tested by the user. The 'what happens if' *and* 'why' scenario does not come as a natural consequence of using all types of software. There is a need for skilful teacher intervention which guides pupils into developing inductive and deductive reasoning, as well as for the careful design of computer software which has sufficient structure to support a discovery approach.

Different mathematical representations of the same or related concepts can be experienced in ways which would not be feasible in a non-computer environment. For example, the computer program Function Graph Plotter could be used to 'solve' the equation $3(x - 1)$ $= x^2 - 1$ by representing different parts of the equation graphically and interpolating the coordinates of the intersections of the two graphs. This would be time consuming and possibly inaccurate by pencil and paper methods. Some different representations of the equation follow; each pair of functions can be graphed and interpreted.

$$y = 3(x - 1) \quad \text{and} \quad y = x^2 - 1$$

$$y = x^2 \quad \text{and} \quad y = 3x - 2$$

$$y = (x^2 - 1)/3 \quad \text{and} \quad y = x - 1$$

$$y = 3x \quad \text{and} \quad y = x^2 + 2$$

$$y = x^2 - 3x + 2 \quad \text{and} \quad y = 0$$

$$y = (x - 1)(x - 2) \quad \text{and} \quad y = 0$$

Changing the problem slightly to 'For what values of x is $3(x - 1) >$ $x^2 - 1$?' immediately invokes the first process function 'conceptual fluency', in the sense that the pupil is freed initially from the difficulties of handling an inequality. It would remain part of the teacher's task to teach towards the skill required in handling inequalities, but only with those for whom it was thought appropriate.

Learning how to learn is an inherent part of the problem-solving process. Learning to learn requires a level of cognition not normally afforded by conventional didactic approaches to teaching. True problem solving will result in a number of paths being followed in an attempt at a solution. Some will be successful, others will not. Conventional pen and paper techniques can of course offer evidence for careful monitoring of various attempts, but it would be an exceptional pupil who would always fully record such attempts and use them to analyse his/her thinking towards a solution. Some software is available which monitors attempts to solve a posed problem. A good example of this is the Micro Electronics Project (MEP) program RAYBOX, originally written with primary pupils in mind but challenging enough to keep secondary pupils (and teachers) thinking hard for quite some time. The problem is to find the location of up to eight 'atoms' hidden in a square grid. Their location can be deduced by observing how a ray (of light) behaves when it is fired into the box. The ray might be deflected through 180° or through a number of 90°

turns, or it might be absorbed (Figure 4.10). Each 'message' indicates possible locations of an atom or atoms. Hypotheses can be tested in practice mode, i.e. with atoms visible, before attempting the real thing. All attempts at locating atoms are recorded and made available when all atoms have been found or when the pupil gives up the attempt. It would take an exceptional pupil at this stage *not* to look at his/her attempts at a solution and learn from what he/she sees.

Figure 4.10 **MEP program RAYBOX showing six atoms and examples of path variations**

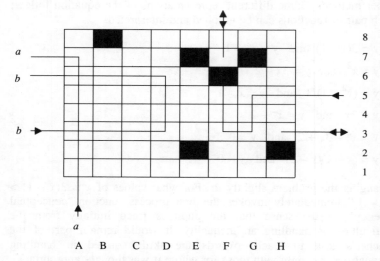

Atoms are found by firing RAYS from around the outside.

If a ray hits an atom it is absorbed.

If a ray tries to pass an atom (in the next row or column) it is sent at right angles as shown and may emerge somewhere else.

If a ray tries to pass between two atoms it is returned.

If a ray enters the box beside an atom it is immediately returned.

Opportunities for role change by the teacher

What is significant about much of the pupils' activities in a computer environment is the very much reduced traditional role of the teacher. It is not by design or a conscious act on the part of the teacher to stay more in the background; it appears the only sensible thing to do under the circumstances which come to prevail. Linked to this role change of the teacher is an equal and opposite role change of the pupil. Comparisons of computer use and conventional instruction reveal from

39 per cent to 88 per cent reduction in the time taken to complete a task (Kulik, *et al.* 1983:24). This may be due to the software itself, how content is presented and solutions pursued, or it may simply be due to an increased work rate by the pupils. A novelty effect may also contribute to an increased work rate. On the face of it there seems to be sufficient evidence to support the use of computers as instructional aids, but we should not overestimate their effectiveness for learning, neither should we equate reduced time on task with an increase in conceptual knowledge (see Chapter 7).

Graphic output and control

To use a microcomputer for learning mathematics only when it is clear that there are no better ways may be an oversimplification in the light of the above comments. The use of computers where there is some control over graphic output is an area where it is difficult to argue that there are any better ways of learning. Functions and their graphs, raw numerical data and bar or pie charts, scatter diagrams or just manipulating shapes all fall into this category. The essence of this work lies in the control which the user has over the computer environment, the control being exercised by the teacher in demonstration mode or by pupils in a workshop mode. Pupils can now draw graphs accurately, superimpose one on another, change parameters to see the effect, zoom in, zoom out, 'see' a limiting behaviour, understand what it is to talk about a point of inflexion. All manner of things can be presented in an interesting way, so that pupils feel that they need to know more about what is going on.

Simulations, microworlds and modelling

It is not possible here to do justice to any one of these powerful implementations, which have enormous potential for the enrichment of learning processes. Each in its own way is capable of offering a computer environment which supports exploration of the user's ideas. Exploration may happen at different levels. The nature of the software and the knowledge domain of the user are likely to determine the kinds of exploration that can take place.

The notion of a computer-based microworld for exploring mathematics in a classroom situation appears to be the most attractive. The attraction lies in the ability to focus upon a limited number of related concepts. Exploration of these concepts can take place without the user having to invest time and effort in overcoming difficulties presented by the computer language used; yet at the same time some access to the computer language is allowed in order to change relationships or rules. It could be argued that a small program such as the one which generates a sequence from a given rule is a microworld in its simplest form. Even this small program allows the user to focus on rules and subsequent patterns, and with a minimum knowledge of a 'language' the user can change those rules; perhaps mathematics is unique in this respect. It is generally agreed that the programming language Logo used in the context of turtle graphics is easy to learn and as such offers pupils even more access in their exploration of a Logo-based microworld. For example, primary school pupils can develop an increased awareness of angle by using a microworld which allows them to focus on the angle through which the turtle turns. The effect produced by the turtle as it moves forward, turns and moves forward again can be matched with other 'angles' presented by the microworld. These user produced angles can then be checked by the system which, in the event of an unacceptable error, can place the pupil at the point where the angle choice can be made again. In this way the microworld can remove some of the difficulties associated with repositioning the turtle and erasing lines, thus allowing the pupil to concentrate on the effect produced by the turtle turning. In this case the teacher has provided the limited framework in which pupils can explore freely. There are, however, other difficulties presented by the use of such microworlds. New difficulties for pupils lie in accommodating their often uncertain ideas about angle with angle as presented by turtle graphics (Simmons and Cope 1990).

Negative factors in computer implementation

Some of the factors at present militating against computers realizing their full potential are:

> lack of expertise in managing the resource
> identification of areas of the curriculum which can be enhanced by the use of computers
> integration into non-computer maths work
> status of mathematical programming and choice of languages.

There is also the very real danger that an overuse of computer algorithms for solving problems will delay or even prevent some of the mathematical thinking we are trying to promote. A balance needs to be maintained between what is explored, appreciated and expressed using computers and how mathematical thinking is encouraged, expressed and refined.

Calculators

Much of the potential of calculators, like that of computers, has yet to be realized. However, unlike computers, calculators containing basic operations and some not so basic are cheap enough to buy in large enough numbers to provide access for all pupils during a mathematics lesson. Much of the reluctance by mathematics teachers to allow the use of the calculator developed from a fear that basic skills in arithmetic would suffer. This fear has now subsided and has been replaced either by a kind of passive indifference to calculator use or by the feeling that more powerful technology in the form of the microcomputer will eventually take over. The author is of the opinion that the accessibility of calculators in their present form offers much in the way of enhancing the mathematics curriculum. The key difference at present between calculators and microcomputers lies in their accessibility for systematic use. It is through systematic use that changes in the mathematics curriculum will be brought about. This systematic use is not yet available with the more attractive microcomputer, but we should not prematurely reject such a powerful tool as the calculator which is available to all pupils on an individual basis.

A large research project (Suydam 1982) has shown that pupils using calculators in mathematics lessons do not lose out on basic skills (this assumes that normal teaching of basic skills continues). In problem solving, pupils were found to score higher when a calculator was used. It proved an effective aid since if it was not known what to do to solve a problem then the presence of a calculator made no difference; if it was known what to do then the use of a calculator was found to make a substantial improvement in problem-solving scores. There were however other important effects: the focus of attention moved from the computational to the strategic; different strategies were used; and more confidence was shown in attempting difficult problems. In areas such as estimation, trigonometry, comparisons with other material aids, retention and transfer, no significant positive effect was found. Out of 36 studies on calculator effects on attitudes towards mathematics, 30 studies found no significant difference and 6 studies showed an improved attitude. However, a later meta-analysis to assess the effects of calculators (Hembree and Dessart 1986:95) found significant positive effects for attitude towards mathematics.

Many of the processes of enrichment made possible by microcomputers can also be tapped using calculators. The gap between calculators and microcomputers in classroom work, for example in exploring number, lies only in the way lessons might be planned and given. Factors such as access for all and the non-requirement for any sophisticated programming skill very much favour the use of the calculator.

Recommendations based on Hembree and Dessart's (1986) research are:

1. Calculators should be used in all mathematics classes.
2. Because of the apparent negative effects of calculators with 8- to

9-year-olds, 'sustained calculator use appears counter-productive with regard to basic skills': (p. 96),calculator functions with this age range should be approached with caution.
3. Students (aged 10 years and older) should be permitted to use calculators in all problem-solving activities, including testing situations. This recommendation is based on two observations:
    (a) Calculators greatly benefit student achievement in problem solving, especially for low- and high-ability students.
    (b) Positive attitudes related to the use of calculators may help to relieve students' traditional dislike of word problems (p. 97).

Using calculators in the classroom

Earlier I mentioned an advantage of calculators over microcomputers, namely that calculators are freely available and lend themselves to systematic use over a long period. If this is to be effective then they must be seen to give the opportunity to do more enjoyable and productive mathematics. This will not necessarily happen by default, and part of the systematic use of calculators should be explicitly planned for by the teacher. Inappropriate use of calculators, for example where mental calculation would be possible and more desirable, can quickly lead to a more endemic situation where their only use is one which substitutes button pressing for thinking. In this sense then the uncritical use of calculators can be counter-productive.

The National Curriculum attainment target 3, number, clearly specifies that for children to attain level 4 they should be able to 'add or subtract mentally 2-digit numbers; add mentally several single-digit numbers; without a calculator add and subtract two 3-digit numbers, multiply a 2-digit number by a single-digit number and divide a 2-digit number by a single-digit number'. Clearly we should avoid any calculator activity which detracts from these basic skills.

For whatever part of the mathematics curriculum we plan to use calculators, we should always be aware of their role in suitably shifting the focus from actually calculating to thinking about the ideas behind the calculation. The ideas of conceptual fluency and mathematical exploration already described in the context of microcomputers apply equally to the use of calculators. Each supports and provides a need for the other. Some ideas follow where conceptual fluency and mathematical exploration can be seen to be working together. At a basic level some of the exercises are simply to allow pupils to become familiar with their particular calculators, but even these can be developed into mathematical exploration and ideas about proof. These exercises are not graded in difficulty and some will require a certain amount of background knowledge.

Playing about with numbers

1. Multiply a number by itself, for example 34×34. Find other ways to use the calculator without entering 34 more than once. (Some calculators will allow 34, $\times$, =, to be pressed, and most will have an x^2 key.)
2. Think of a way in which you can find all four-digit square numbers of the form *xxyy*, 3399 is a number of this form but it is not square! Some concepts which may be invoked in the process of finding a solution are:
    (a) that 1100 is the smallest such number
    (b) that 9999 is the largest such number
    (c) that $10 \times 10 = 100$ and not 1000
    (d) that $30 \times 30 = 900$
    (e) that 33 multiplied by itself is the smallest number to try
    (f) the idea of a square root of a number
    (g) that we need only look for numbers beginning 11--, 22--, 33-- etc.
3. Multiply any two two-digit numbers together. Do this about ten times and write down the results, e.g.

    $23 \times 13 = 299$
    $45 \times 26 = 1170$
    . . .

    All the numbers on the right-hand side are composite numbers, and each has at least two factors other than the number itself and 1.
4. Try to find whole numbers which multiply together to make 73, other than 73×1. A number which does not have factors other than the number itself and 1 is a prime number. How can you improve your test for a prime number? Some concepts which may be invoked are:
    (a) that when looking for factors we need not look any further than the square root of the number
    (b) that any number can be written as a product of prime factors
    (c) that it is sufficient to test for all prime factors less than or equal to the square root of the number
    (d) the idea of making a table of prime numbers
    (e) the idea of generating a table of prime numbers by using the sieve of Eratosthenes.

Practical tasks

The following is influenced by Parker and Straker (1989).

Kepler's work on planetary orbits in 1609 had necessitated the calculation of areas based on the idea of infinitely small triangles as shown in Figure 4.11. The idea was a forerunner of the idea of integral calculus. He developed this line of thinking for calculating the volumes of objects where no formula was known. His method was based on the generation of solids of revolution by rotating familiar shaped areas about an axis. For example a 'citron' (Figure 4.12) and an 'apple' (Figure 4.13) are generated by rotating respectively a minor and a major segment of a circle about its chord. Each shape was then sliced into elemental discs of varying radii which when added together approximated the original volume.

Figure 4.11 **Triangular elemental areas in planetary orbit**

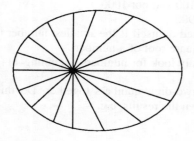

Figure 4.12 **A citron**

'The year 1612 had been a very good year for wine', so the history books tell us, and it was during this year that Kepler applied his volume finding technique to wine barrels. One would expect the error involved in finding the volume of a barrel to be less than that of a citron, given the same slice thickness. (Can you suggest why this might be so?)

Figure 4.13 **An apple**

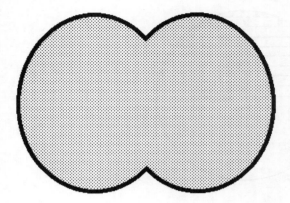

This technique can be used effectively to establish well known but little understood formulae of objects like the sphere and the cone, which can be treated with a simple step-by-step method of calculation aided by a calculator. For example the volume of a sphere is $\frac{4}{3}\pi r^3$ and the surface area of a sphere is $4\pi r^2$. This activity fits in well with the National Curriculum attainment target 9, using and applying mathematics, levels 7–10. Level 7 states: 'Devise a mathematical task; work methodically within an agreed structure; use judgement in the use of given information; use "trial and improvement" methods; review progress.'

The structure of the mathematical task for finding volume is as suggested by Parker and Straker (1989); a strategy for finding surface area is added. For the volume:

1. Choose a suitable radius for the sphere (here 4).
2. Draw a full-size cross-section through the centre of the sphere.
3. Decide how to split up your sphere: how many slices?
4. Measure the radius of each slice (take half the minimum diameter, this will be zero for the final slice).
5. Find the volume of each disc.

Figure 4.14 shows the sphere with one half divided into discs. Table 4.1 shows the volume calculation. The sum of the final column in the table represents half the volume V of the sphere; hence the volume of the sphere is approximated by 247.38. So we can make the conjecture that for some K,

$V = K\pi r^3$ (r^3 since we are dealing with volume)
and for $r = 4$,
$K = 247.38/\pi 4^3 = 1.23$

Figure 4.14 **Finding the volume of a sphere**

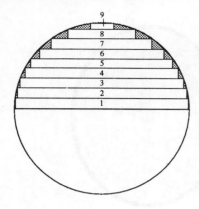

Table 4.1 **Calculating the volume of one half of a sphere**

No. of disc	Radius of disc r	Thickness of disc h	Volume of disc $\pi r^2 h$
1	3.95	0.5	24.508
2	3.9	0.5	23.892
3	3.7	0.5	21.504
4	3.45	0.5	18.696
5	3.15	0.5	15.586
6	2.7	0.5	11.451
7	2.0	0.5	6.283
8	1.4	0.25	1.539
9	0.7	0.15	0.231
			123.690

Since the estimated volume is less than the actual volume, we can state with certainty that the true value of K is a little more than 1.23. More calculations would be needed in order to arrive at the value of about 4/3, i.e. the 'trial and improvement' referred to in AT9 level 7.

An improvement in the method of calculation would be the realization that we need only calculate r^2 for each disc of equal thickness (discs 1–7), place the cumulative sum in calculator memory and multiply by πh, and then add on the volumes of the smaller discs (i.e. 121.920 + 1.770 = 123.690).

Improvements in choosing a way of dividing up the sphere would be:

reducing the disc thickness, say by half
using a mid-point of each disc's side to compensate for the gaps caused by the first method

using discs which take more volume than necessary in order to create an upper bound.

It will have become clear that although the division of a sphere into discs provides us with a fairly accurate estimate for the volume, the same arrangement for calculating surface area fails rather badly. This is easy to see why. In Figure 4.14 the fit of the curved surface of each disc is only a good one for discs 1 and 2, and thereafter it becomes rather poor; so another type of division is necessary. Figure 4.15 shows a division again based on discs, but this time discs whose curved surface is curved in two directions. This results in discs of varying thickness determined by radii at 10° intervals; the curved surfaces of the discs closely approximate the curved surface of the sphere. Each arc length of type BC in Figure 4.15 is $(10/360) \times 2\pi r = 2\pi/9$ (where $r = 4$).

Figure 4.15 **Finding the surface area of a sphere. ABCO represents half of disc 1**

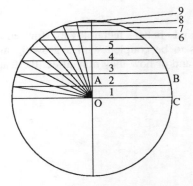

Table 4.2 shows the surface area calculation. The sum of the final column represents half the surface area s of the sphere. As can be seen, this sum can be obtained more concisely as

$$s/2 = 23.3 \times 2\pi/9 \times 2\pi = 102.205$$

Thus $s = 204.41$. So for some K,

$s = Kr^2 = 204.41$ (r^2 since we are dealing with area)
$K = 204.41/r^2 = 204.41/16 = 12.7756$
$K/\pi = 12.7756/\pi = 4.066$

So we can conjecture that surface area is $4\pi r^2$.

Enriching the process of learning then can take many forms, and can be actively pursued by all teachers and experienced by all pupils. The

Table 4.2 **Calculating the area of one half of a sphere**

No. of disc	Mean radius of disc r	Length of curved surface h	Curved surface area of disc $2\pi rh$
1	4	$2\pi/9$	17.546
2	3.9	$2\pi/9$	17.107
3	3.65	$2\pi/9$	16.011
4	3.3	$2\pi/9$	14.475
5	2.9	$2\pi/9$	12.721
6	2.3	$2\pi/9$	10.089
7	1.8	$2\pi/9$	7.896
8	1.1	$2\pi/9$	4.825
9	0.35	$2\pi/9$	1.535
	23.3		102.205

emergence of better and better technologies for enhancing the educative process needs to be coupled with a growing awareness of possible classroom uses and of how they may affect the teacher's role.

CHAPTER 5

Communication, language and mathematics

'One of the nicest questions to be asked by a pupil is 'Can I try and say that, because I don't think I can?' (Mason and Pimm 1986:33)

The communication of mathematical ideas in the classroom takes place through various forms of language. This may be spoken or written, formal or informal, between pupils and teacher or between pupil and pupil. The main focus of this chapter is on the spoken word and how it may be used to bring about mathematical understanding as a practical alternative to the rigours imposed by following the purely symbolic approach found all too frequently in secondary mathematics classrooms. After all in many real world problem-solving situations an understanding of a problem is developed by talking with others who have an interest in its solution.

In the initial stages of problem solving, talk is likely to be unfocused and lacking in precision as participants try to come to terms with new ideas and attempt to piece together a solution framework which eventually might be more succinctly expressed in symbolic notation. The importance which many mathematics educators attach to encouraging this to happen in secondary mathematics classrooms is captured in the following quotation: 'One focal concern of all involved in mathematics education should be to ascertain how to deny symbols pride of place as the objects of mathematical enquiry, a place they have the tendency to usurp by default' (Pimm 1987:203).

Pimm is not asking us to deny mathematics the very real power derived from being able to work with symbols at a representational level, but merely to delay their use until proper meanings have been negotiated. At the representational level laws connecting symbols allow the user to develop ideas without dragging along an in-depth meaning at each stage of the development. However, the ability to work at a level of generalization or to demonstrate that certain skills can be applied may or may not imply that some basic understanding has already been achieved. We need, therefore, to begin at the beginning and consider the place of language in mathematics classrooms.

Austin and Howson (1979:163) make the distinction between the language of the learner, the language of the teacher and the language of mathematics, but quickly point out that 'no clear-cut classification exists'. However, such a classification serves to highlight the needs and responsibilities of pupils, teachers and all who communicate mathematics.

The language used by the learner can happen at two levels, firstly as an internal process most frequently evoked when coming to terms with a new concept or when the learner's existing structures are found to be inadequate, and secondly functioning externally to communicate ideas to others. Thinking aloud appears to be a very necessary part of concept formation and concept development, particularly in younger children. Piaget (1928) described this as egocentric talk – talk through which there is a striving for internal consistency of meaning for the benefit of the individual and no one else. Piaget also recognized the social aspects of talk, not least the ability to listen and appreciate another person's point of view. Hoyles (1985) distinguishes between the cognitive function of talk and the communicative function of talk: 'the cognitive function for the articulation of one's own thought processes, and the communicative function for making one's ideas available to another' (p. 206). Brown (1982:77) describes the communicative function as defined by Hoyles as having two parts. She describes these two aspects of pupil talk as message oriented speech and listener oriented speech; the former demands communication skills which are not a natural outcome of exposure to situations where discussion takes place. The successful outcome of message oriented speech, i.e. that the listener understands the message, according to Brown and reported by Pimm (1987), 'involves a more efficient packing of information, a more structured delivery with more syntactic marking' (p. 40). Hoyles (1985) similarly characterizes the 'communicative function' of talk arising from a situation where there is a need to share ideas as identifying 'those parts of a mathematical situation seen as important for meaning and those that are not, and how the former relate to one another' (p. 206).

The different levels of understanding as articulated by Skemp (1971) can also be viewed from a 'talk' perspective. At the level of instrumental understanding there seems little to talk about, since the procedure to reach a solution is 'known'; there is no questioning and no conflict. However, Pirie (1988) suggests that even though a child shows a rule-based solution it does not necessarily mean that a deeper understanding of the concepts does not exist.

In acquiring relational understanding, i.e. understanding for oneself, some internalization of concepts will have taken place. Skemp (1971:65) sees the cognitive function of talk as part of the process of developing reflective intelligence. Barnes (1976:28) describes this as exploratory talk through which one's own thoughts are developed and ideas refined. The communicative function may be linked to logical understanding, i.e. the ability to convince others, which can come about only if there are others around to listen and be convinced. Hoyles (1985) points out that attempting to convince others requires clear identification of the salient points of a mathematical situation and that in a group situation more thoughtful use of language is required to convey meaning. Barnes (1976:113) describes this as final-draft talk where criteria external to the learner's needs come into play.

Pirie and Schwarzenberger (1988:461) define mathematical discussion as 'purposeful talk on a mathematical subject in which there are genuine pupil contributions and interaction'. Many researchers into classroom talk are agreed that very little mathematical discussion as defined above actually takes place in classrooms. It is also clear from my own experience of students learning to teach that there is confusion in their minds about what discussion really is. This is not surprising since it is unlikely that they have witnessed much discussion as defined above either as a pupil or as a student teacher. Very often students use the word 'discussion' in their lesson planning to indicate a period of questions and answers to be led from the front by the teacher. These exchanges by student teachers are often characterized by their brevity, by the preponderance of lower-order or closed questions being asked, and by the acceptance of pupil responses which match the teacher's own ideas and the rejection of those that do not. In no sense can these exchanges be described as discussion. It may be, however, that teachers who genuinely want to develop discussion in their classrooms can change the nature of these exchanges so that the climate is more conducive to purposeful discussion.

For instance, consider the effect of the teacher evaluating a response from a pupil not from a mathematical point of view but only procedurally. It seems more likely, but is not guaranteed, that in this situation other pupils will continue to be involved because the teacher's acknowledgement of the first pupil's response has not closed down all other thinking. Indeed it may also allow for the first pupil to have second thoughts and express them. The nature of responses by the pupils may also be less restricted if they find that they do not have to second-guess the teacher. Responses are more likely to be founded on thinking about the mathematics and the problem. Clarification of ideas, alternative ideas and even task-related questions may also come from the pupils. When this happens, teacher-led question and answer becomes teacher-led discussion.

The procedural skills required and the time available with any one group in order to bring this about may be beyond those engaged in teaching practice. Attention must of course be paid to establishing ground rules by which any effective classroom has to operate. Attempts to move from a tightly led question and answer situation to more open discussion will be seen to work against classroom order. In order to keep open discussion going so that all can benefit, attention needs to be given to:

how contributors are cued to speak
how contributors indicate that they want to speak
keeping discussion flowing without too many silences or
interruptions
skilful monitoring of contributions
linking and developing suggested ideas.

Working simultaneously with this procedural process is the
development of a mathematical situation. Each affects and is affected
by the other. Brissenden (1988:115) indicates how the nature of the
mathematics and the aims being pursued by the teacher determine the
extent to which discussion is directed and focused by the teacher.
Aims dealing with facts, skills and conceptual structures are likely to
invoke teacher directed goals, whereas the development of general
strategies and personal qualities through exploratory activities leads to
more open discussions. The teacher's role in the latter two cases is still
procedural but less evaluative. The teacher's role is also less
authoritative as the teacher acts as an honest broker in negotiating
meaning between pupils; pupils themselves largely determine the
course of events. There is a reduced tendency for the teacher to listen
for those responses which develop his/her own ideas about the
problem situation.

Practical considerations

This book is about ways of making mathematics teaching and learning
in secondary classrooms more effective. Much of the research into the
value of discussions in bringing about mathematical understanding has
concentrated on primary classrooms. This is understandably so since it
is widely believed that younger children have a greater need to
verbalize in order to comprehend. It is the author's view that much can
be learned from research into discussion at primary school level and
applied within a secondary context. Mathematics teaching at secondary
school is characterized, perhaps more than any other subject, by its
lack of discussion. There are many reasons for this, some already
explained in other parts of this book. There is an overwhelming
tendency for the traditional view of mathematics teaching to be passed
on from one generation of teachers to another. Perhaps the notions
about teaching gained as a pupil remain resistant to later influences in
initial and in-service training. It may also be that research into new
classroom approaches fails for one reason or another to bring about a
lasting change in the way we view mathematics and consequently how
we teach it. Practical guidelines based on sound research findings
which appear to work would seem to be a reasonable way forward.
Part of the problem lies in the fact that in order to get things moving

in a practical way some simplification of the situation, as revealed by research, has to take place, and any general claims are tempered by local knowledge and at times gut reaction. In this sense teachers in daily contact with pupils in ordinary classroom situations are uniquely placed to experiment and monitor new (for them) approaches to teaching a mathematical topic. This may be founded on nothing but a hunch which may or may not be supported by previous research.

The case for encouraging discussion in mathematics at any level appears on the whole to be a strong one. Various conjectures support the idea, such as:

Having students work together appears to enhance the class environment and social interaction, and increases learning that takes place. We have a hunch it could help with overcoming bugs or getting at problems underneath. For instance, having students show each other what they are doing might help them to articulate their strategies. Teachers would thereby gain access to these strategies, and the students themselves would become aware that their strategies may differ from those of other students. The development of metacognition would be aided. (Maurer 1987:179)

We thus get 'two for the price of one', timewise. The children learn mathematics better and the teachers learn about the intelligent learning of mathematics by observing their own children in the process.' (Skemp 1985 :8)

Others are more cautious:

We hope that our observations and analysis will lead to recommendations for future research, but at this stage we can neither substantiate nor deny the attractive hypothesis of a causal relationship between mathematical discussion and mathematical understanding. (Pirie and Schwarzenberger 1988:469)

This last quotation comments on a preliminary analysis of whether or not discussion in the mathematics classroom is an aid to understanding. This ongoing research seeks to answer three important questions about mathematical discussion:

1. What is it that gives the speakers something to talk about?
2. What level of language is being used?
3. What kind of statements are being made?

What is clear so far is that the answers to these questions can vary within any one discussion episode. For example, an understanding of the next stage of a problem would lead to statements being made about how to proceed, but a lack of understanding about the next stage would lead to more reflective or exploratory statements being made.

There can of course be no guarantees that certain topics or processes in mathematics will generate discussion. The teacher well acquainted with handling discussion in the classroom could no doubt generate discussion about any aspect of mathematics. This seems to suggest that the teacher's view of mathematics is more influential on classroom processes than the choice of mathematics. Mason and Pimm (1986) endorse this idea and suggest how the subject of discussion could lie within any of the following:

mathematical techniques
definitions
results
standard errors
contradictions
generalizations
mathematical processes
mental imagery
computer programs.

It seems to me that success in any one of the above areas crucially depends upon the teacher's leadership and ability to see and promote different yet connected ideas. Take, for example, what many student teachers describe as a fairly uninspiring topic, 'gradient'. This could fall under the headings of mathematical techniques and definitions, and could quite easily stay rooted there throughout a number of lessons under the heading 'gradient'. If this were the case then the equation (definition?)

$$\text{gradient} = \frac{\text{vertical distance (up or down)}}{\text{horizontal distance}}$$

would remain central to the processes of finding gradients or unknown distances. It would be unlikely that pupils working within such a regime would appreciate the meaning of gradient and be aware of the many aspects of mathematics which relate to it.

Consider the effect of introducing, by question, illustration or other stimulus, the following connected notions:

1. We see 15 per cent on a roadside signpost: What does it mean? How can we handle it mathematically?
2. What simplifications do we make by drawing right-angled triangles to illustrate how this might relate to the number 15?
3. Averages? What do we mean by average slope between two points?
4. Percentages?
5. Fractions? Equivalent fractions?
6. How many different 'hills' can you think of which have a gradient of 15 per cent?
7. Similar triangles?
8. Ratio?

9. What does it mean to have a gradient greater than one? Do these exist? Can you draw one?
10. What could we mean by a negative gradient? What would it look like? Downhill? Uphill? Do these really exist? Can you draw one?

Trying to bring a number of these notions into play at any one time requires some of the pupil and teacher skills to which I have already referred, but also begs various questions. How should we organize pupils in order to encourage exploration, free expression and effective communication of ideas? What can we expect from a pupil learning point of view? Can we predict what aspects of a situation are likely to lead to the kinds of interaction thought to improve achievement?

Learning and sharing mathematics in small groups

In concluding this brief chapter it would seem appropriate to discuss some of the research findings related to pupil interaction and achievement when pupils are organized into small groups. For our purposes here a small group would typically be from two to five members. Many of the findings are related to learning in general in small groups but almost all the studies reported here have some element of mathematics as content. Since investigative approaches to the teaching of mathematics continue to gain ground, an improved understanding of some of the complex processes involved with group work assumes a greater relevance for practising teachers, particularly for those teachers who wish to plan for and encourage more exploratory talk within small groups.

Using a group approach to look at mathematics investigatively might be viewed as just another way of completing a task; the more heads working, the sooner the task will be done. It may be seen as an expedient way in which to complete 'an investigation' within a given 40 minutes. Viewing group work strictly in this way is to deny other possibilities for learning mathematics and for learning to work as a group. The focus of group work can be on improving learning through pupil interaction and on improving the learning environment. Central to this idea is the nature of pupil interaction and how it can be evoked and sustained.

In an extensive review of research in this area, Webb (1982) focuses on three aspects of small group learning:

the relationship between interaction and achievement
the cognitive and social aspects of group work which link interaction with achievement
the predictors of interaction.

It should be stated that not all researchers have found group work to be beneficial for learning. In certain circumstances individual, competitive working has proved more beneficial. However the bulk of evidence, although not entirely consistent, indicates that much can be gained by encouraging interaction within groups. Some of the reasons for these inconsistencies are given in a later work by Webb (1983).

Figure 5.1 indicates the ideas central to learning within small groups. The types and quality of the links between the fertile situations (discussed in Chapter 4) and the kinds of interaction which take place inevitably depend upon the teacher's perception of the process and his/her role within it.

Figure 5.1 **Learning in small groups**

Ideas put forward in the Williams (1970) model discussed in Chapter 4 can be linked with the input-interaction-achievement system described by Webb (1982). In the Williams model (Figure 4.1), dimension 1 (subject matter content) and dimension 2 (teacher behaviour) can be thought of as inputs for creating the right situations. Dimension 3 (pupil behaviours) can be considered as being part of the interaction between pupils and part of the necessary processes, cognitive and affective, which turn active engagement into learning and achievement.

Barnes (1976:Appendix) lists five important factors for effective group organization to which I add my own brief interpretation:

1. Feeling of competence by pupils: this is an outcome of the composition of groups and the pupils' perception of the teacher's role in the whole process.
2. Common ground: pupils' abilities to restate and reorganize presented situations into representations they can all share; the use of language at the pupils' level is all important at this stage.
3. Focusing: the teacher's ability to present a problem framework which provides the kind of help needed to start pupils thinking and to start asking their own relevant questions.
4. Pace: basically allowing time for exploratory talk to take place; again a balance is required between allowing time for learning to take place and time to show that the job has been done.

5. Making public: The need to refine language appropriate to a wider audience. For example, groups reporting back to the whole class would require a spokesperson to collect and present the findings of the group using more explicit language so that other groups less familiar with the situation can appreciate the points being made. This is a more demanding stage requiring firmness and understanding on the part of the teacher, since the teacher's presence is likely to induce the feeling that explicitness is not required.

Although some studies have found positive relationships between interaction and achievement, the picture presented is a mixed one. What becomes clearer in the later study by Webb (1983) is that the variety and form of language used is fundamental to the quality of interaction which takes place. Earlier studies on interaction within groups took account only of the quantity of all types of interaction between pupils, or grouped together all kinds of helping behaviour within the group. In the former case interaction was found not to relate to achievement; in the latter case, where helping behaviour and achievement were correlated, results were mixed (Webb 1983:34). Other studies where rewards for group achievements were given were more consistent, finding in the majority of cases that there was a positive relationship between helping other pupils and achievement.

Further studies which distinguished between giving and receiving help found evidence that giving help was positively related to achievement for low-ability pupils but not for average or high-ability pupils (Webb 1983:34). A further distinction between three types of help – conceptual/sequencing explanations, giving directions and giving answers – was made by Swing and Peterson (1982). Their study of pupils working in small groups on division and fractions over a four-week period revealed that giving explanations by pupils had a positive effect on achievement in both areas for those of low-ability and in division for high-ability pupils; that receiving explanations had a positive effect on achievement in fraction work for low-ability pupils; that receiving directions had a positive effect on achievement in division work for low-ability pupils; and that receiving answers only had the most profound negative effect on achievement across all groups (p. 269).

A snapshot of this rather complicated research area demonstrates the inconsistencies found in some of the earlier work. As research into this area has progressed, greater cognizance has been made of the type of help given and received by pupils working in small groups. An analysis by Webb has shown that certain types of giving and receiving help have a negative effect on achievement. For example, she found that 'receiving terminal responses had nearly as great [a negative] impact on achievement as receiving no response' (Webb 1983:38).

Factors such as these could well have resulted in the inconsistencies found in earlier work; that is, by not distinguishing between the type of help being given and received, the various competing effects of such help would be likely to lead to results which say nothing very much. However, in summarizing helping in small groups, it does appear to be the case that

1. Giving explanations by pupils is beneficial.
2. Giving correct answers by pupils or just pointing out errors has little effect on achievement.
3. Receiving explanations is also beneficial, particularly in response to a specific need, and more generally for low attainers.
4. Receiving terminal responses or no response to a request for help is detrimental to achievement.
5. Passive behaviour and behaviour not related to the task show a negative but non-significant relationship with achievement.

However in all this analysis there is the important act of pupil talk and its effect on achievement. It was thought that merely talking about mathematics in group work would increase achievement; however, research which tested performance of pupils in different interactive settings, for example talking with pupils as opposed to talking with teachers or researchers, has indicated that the *purpose* of talk is more important for learning than the act of talking. Pupils talking with pupils out-performed those pupils talking with teachers. There is yet further evidence that verbalizing to teach rather than just explaining is even more performance enhancing. Those of us who regularly go through this process will need little convincing that some restructuring of our knowledge takes place both during preparation of material for lessons and during the interaction of giving lessons. Pupil–pupil interaction of this kind will no doubt result in some similar restructuring on the part of the 'teacher' and 'taught', with the possible advantage of both speaking the same verbal and non-verbal language.

Another important factor influencing the effectiveness of group work is the reward structure which is in operation. A detailed analysis of four well researched models is given in Slavin (1980:319). The models essentially present different reward structures based on group cooperation where individual success can have a greater or lesser influence upon the success of the whole group. What seems vital for the successful application of any reward structure, from a motivational point of view, is that the success of each individual is recognized and has some explicit contribution to the success of the group. Other factors which influence interaction within groups (Webb 1982:431) and which may act as predictors of pupil behaviour are:

the individual ability of the pupil

the composition of groups according to ability
whether pupils are or are not encouraged to work with others
whether individual or group achievements are compared with the
achievements of other individuals or groups.

Research has indicated that helping behaviour occurred less frequently
in homogeneous high-ability and low-ability groups, and in general
there was more helping given in response to need in heterogeneous
groups.

In summary, Webb concludes:

Student interaction may be partially predicted from characteristics of the
individual and of the group, and reward structure. Of all the predictors
examined here, student ability and reward structure had the most consistent
relations with student interaction. High-ability students gave more explanations
than low-ability students. Rewarding students for the achievement of all group
members consistently promoted helping behaviour. (1982: 438)

Bennett and Desforges's (1985) account of research into classroom
grouping is perhaps less optimistic than that presented here in how it
sees theory being put into practice. They conclude:

The reality of groups as currently organized is generally a physical
juxtaposition of individual pupils operating without clear purpose or adequate
management. As such cooperation is limited and rarely task enhancing, and
off-task interaction is frequent and often inadvertently encouraged by lack of
supervision. Such classroom groups are unlikely to be effective vehicles for
efficient learning . . . Group discussion methods may be more appropriate
for the development of higher-order skills and for certain types of classroom
task. For the development and practice of basic skills, on the other hand, the
incorporation of an incentive system would seem more appropriate. This
implies that teachers need to carefully consider the most appropriate learning
setting in relation to their aims and intentions. (p. 116)

CHAPTER 6

Investigative mathematics through problem solving

Whole books have been written on the subject of mathematical problem solving. Some concentrate on techniques for solving problems, others on pedagogy, a few on human cognition and related research; yet more aim to present interesting problems and share the experience of finding solutions. Problem solving has always been at the centre of mathematics; it just seems that each new generation has to discover for themselves its central role.

George Polya's book *How to Solve It*, first published in 1945, has a lot to say for today's problem solvers, which may indicate that there are certain unchanging truths within the bedrock of problem-solving techniques. The last decade has seen some genuine and successful attempts to develop across mathematics teaching Polya's perspective that mathematics through problem solving is accessible to all. The aim of this chapter is to give the reader a first look across the scene of mathematical problem solving, and as such to dip into its various aspects. The reader is left to decide for him/herself which of these aspects are more important.

What is mathematical problem solving?

Problem solving is mathematics in the making. (House 1980:157)

Schoolchildren seldom see much of this face of mathematics; for them, the construction scaffolding has been taken away, and all that remains is the completed edifice through which they are guided. (Kilpatrick 1985:3)

After some reflection on these statements one is bound to ask the question: is the solution of standard textbook problems really mathematics in the making? One might answer: it depends upon the problem (Kilpatrick 1985:4) and how the solver goes about achieving a solution.

A typical textbook word problem requiring a single operation on the only two numbers given in the problem is I suppose problem solving of a kind, but compared with the kinds of experience a more open form of enquiry can bring, it is a bit like trying to see the world by just standing still. So as teachers it is important if we wish to promote real problem-solving activity in our classrooms to actively search for and research the types of problems with which pupils can identify and which they wish to solve. This means that teachers too have to become active problem solvers, drawing not only on their mathematics expertise but also on their knowledge of classrooms and pupils as problem solvers. The process of solving the problems will then be enhanced partly by the pupils' own motivations and partly by the actions of the teacher in encouraging pupils towards a solution.

In a paper presented in 1949, Polya describes as 'the great opportunity of mathematics' the unique combination of favouring circumstances which allows mathematical problems to be solved by average ability pupils on a scientific level. Behind this idea is the implication that problem solving is not a spectator sport, nor is it necessarily the matching of acquired knowledge to new situations; it is a searching for a solution by actions which seem appropriate.

This, one might argue, presupposes that the solver has a clearly conceived aim; as Shulman (1985) points out, the 'task-environment' as perceived by the teacher is not necessarily the same as the 'problem space' as perceived by the pupil. It is suggested by Shulman, and others, that before a mathematical problem can be identified as such, and as having a solution attainable through the use of mathematics, there are two stages of refinement to which the real problem solver must be predisposed. These are, firstly, the encounter with a situation which leaves the solver with a vague feeling about what he/she has experienced and some discomfort in *not* knowing what is *not* known; and secondly, to come to terms with what is not known and impose a structure which changes a troubled situation into a well conceived problem.

Figure 6.1 **Problem-solving process**

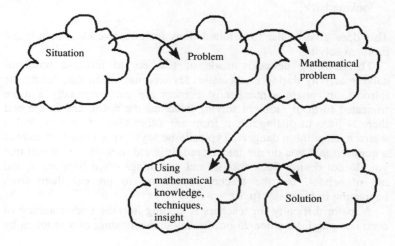

The subsequent identification of the mathematics which describes the problem and which can be used to develop a solution is part of the *mathematical* problem-solving process. Where more open problem solving in mathematics classrooms takes place it does so largely from this third stage where the mathematics of the problem has been clearly identified by the problem setter. Indeed, much of the research into mathematical problem solving concentrates its efforts towards understanding the processes which take place after the problem has been defined in a mathematical way.

Figure 6.1 represents a simplified view of problem solving in both scope and detail. There are those who point out that solvers of *real* problems have to live through the consequences of their actions (solutions) and are required to evaluate their success by reference to initial conditions rather than to surface features of a simplified mathematical model. It is difficult to see how these two additional stages of the problem-solving process can be imposed effectively in a classroom situation. Classroom situations, although part of the real world, can mostly only simulate or represent real situations, with the consequent dilution of responsibility and accountability (but see later for accountability).

It may be that we have to settle for coming to terms with a limited form of problem solving when the practicalities of teaching demand certain measurable levels of skill, understanding and application. That there is value in this more restricted view of problem solving is demonstrated by no less a teacher than Polya (1945:xvi) himself. He offers a four-stage model of mathematical problem solving:

understanding the problem
devising a plan
carrying out the plan
looking back.

This does give us the firm foundations for effective classroom-based problem solving.

The growing demands made of teachers to increase problem-solving activity during mathematics lessons may mean that during the introductory phase a number of corners are cut, eventually a more truncated form of problem solving becomes the norm, and in the end there is little to distinguish it from any other kind of activity. Polya warns against these dangers. Typically he says: 'It is foolish to answer a question that you do not understand. It is sad to work for an end that you do not desire. Such foolish and sad things often happen, in and out of school, but the teacher should try to prevent them from happening in his class' (p. 6).

A major difficulty for teachers is tapping into the understanding of even one pupil, let alone 25 or 30. Any understanding of a problem by a pupil can be measured only indirectly by observing how a pupil consciously links his/her own plan or algorithm to the problem domain. The difficulties which pupils have in communicating a plan of action to others must mean that we can expect to get only a partial picture of any pupil's understanding. Actually devising a plan, including false trails, and communicating it to others is an essential part of problem solving and must not be confused with the recall of algorithms triggered by half-remembered associations. The former can create new solution paths based on different representations of a problem, the latter can at best produce a single correct solution. The former is mathematics in the making, the latter is the undoing of mathematical thinking.

The problem-solving stages in Figure 6.1 from a pedagogical point of view can range from a situation where problem, solution path and solutions are all given, to a 'pure inquiry' situation where not even the problem is defined (Shulman 1985:440). Between these two relatively rare extremes lie the more popular problem formats where the problem is given as a situation, word problem and/or diagram; solution paths are not given, or are perhaps hinted at or even explicitly laid down; and the solutions are not given. Using these different problem formats allows for variation in the amount of teacher control of the area of study, and have been part and parcel of mathematics education through the ages.

It must be remembered that under these circumstances the motivation of the solver may only be of a secondary nature in the sense that a task has been set by the teacher and some attempt at a solution is expected. Further motivation may develop as a result of early success or by finding some familiarity with the mathematics, but the primary motivation of wanting to solve the problem may not be there. The 'pure inquiry' approach involves greater risk but has potentially greater rewards, not least that some primary motivation lies behind the solver's energies in solving his/her own problem.

Posing one's own problems has a number of advantages for the pupil:

1. Not everyone will have a quick answer (this includes the teacher).
2. It will be difficult for others to judge a pupil's performance when solving an unfamiliar problem; this will reduce anxiety levels and promote more reflective thought.
3. Reflective thought may lead to a solution or to a problem modification (pupils are on the whole reluctant to modify a problem set by the teacher).
4. Problem modification may lead to a greater understanding of the original problem.
5. Problem modification may lead to further questions being asked and subproblems being defined (the cycle is complete).

Teaching problem solving

It is noticeable that in discussing problem solving one is almost compelled to talk about its teaching. The act of problem solving draws upon all aspects of the educational scene. Its central position is not disputed, nor is its potential for changing mathematics teaching. Finding access to and harnessing such potential needs to be a primary aim of all those involved in mathematics education. We might ask if the amount of time we devote to problem solving is consistent with our admission of its importance. One lesson out of seven or eight per week would appear not to support the argument that we take problem solving seriously. It would seem that improved frequency and quality of problem solving should be our targets in our attempt to reform what we do.

Two major areas of development appear to be important if these targets are to be met. The first is to decide what we mean by problem solving and how it manifests itself in the classroom. The second is to determine those aspects of pedagogy which allow it to happen and enhance its quality. In deciding what kind of problem solving we want to encourage we have to consider what kinds of strategies pupils find useful in solving problems and whether strategic thinking can be taught effectively. We have to decide on the types of problems we ought to set in order to build in the necessary variety and depth of experience. We have to recognize the potential of discussion in problem solving (see Chapter 5). Our choice of teaching approach will depend upon the importance we give to establishing a problem-solving climate and which teaching strategies and organizational strategies we consider to be effective for the integration of problem solving into the mathematics curriculum.

Strategies

What kind of problem-solving strategies should we attempt to teach? Whatever strategies we do attempt to teach we must be careful not to give the impression that this is something different, that this kind of thinking is parcelled up and applies only to an activity called problem solving. It is easy to present this detached image to children, whereby they see 'doing maths' as a separate activity requiring a different response from that demanded by problem solving. Whatever strategies we put forward they should aim for long term growth in the variety of problems which pupils are willing to attempt.

As a start we can consider putting forward some general guidelines based on our own experiences and the experiences of others in solving problems. Most books on problem solving give a variety of these guidelines but there is a large degree of agreement on the principles involved. It is in the interpretation of guidelines that differences appear. Four different texts on problem solving have been selected; their guidelines for problem solving are given in Table 6.1. Some have been paraphrased, others have been much shortened for comparison purposes.

Table 6.1 **Guidelines for problem solving**

Burton (1984)	Gardiner (1987)	Schoenfeld (1980) (a)	Dolan and Williamson (1983)
Entry	Guess intelligently Test your guesses	Understand the problem	Guess and check
Attack	Look for connections Identify subproblems	Design a solution	Make a table
Review	Try to prove	Verify the solution	Spot patterns Use a model
Extension	Apply results and methods to answer related questions	Explore solutions to difficult problems	Simplify Eliminate

Each of these sets of guidelines has its own more detailed heuristics except for that of Dolan and Williamson (1983), which appears to concentrate on strategies which may help progress towards the solution, and could be thought of as a more detailed account of the attack phase. The usefulness of each subset will depend on the type of problem being solved and the knowledge of the solver. For example, drawing a diagram for solving the triangle problem given later is, I would suggest, a more useful strategy than guessing and checking, although the act of checking may well involve drawing a diagram. Likewise it is unlikely that 'argue by contradiction or contrapositive' is going to be useful advice for the average 12-year-old, regardless of the type of problem being solved. Therefore to choose a strategy appropriate for the problem and to apply the strategy at a level which the user can appreciate are crucial steps. Some examples are given later, but for the moment consider the following problem.

Problem: cutting a shape to form a square

The problem is to cut the shape in figure 6.2 into four pieces with two straight cuts, so that the four pieces, when put together in a certain way, will form a perfect square. The square must have no overlapping pieces and no gaps. You may find what follows more meaningful if you pause at this stage and try to solve the problem yourself. The use of squared paper and a pair of scissors may help. You can then compare your solution with that presented here.

*Figure 6.2 **Shape for dissection***

Understanding the problem

At first the problem seems rather difficult and one gets the feeling that any early success is going to be because we got lucky. A likely initial strategy would be to draw some images of the figure on squared paper, make two straight cuts which produce four pieces and try to fit them together to form a square. Success at this stage, however unlikely, is going to be unproductive, simply because thinking about the problem has not begun. So where next? What does the problem say?

1.   Four pieces have to fit together to form a square.
2.   Two cuts only are allowed.

What do these two statements taken together actually tell us?

Attacking the problem

We can say at least three things at this stage:

1.   Each of the four pieces has to have a right angle which can represent the corner of a square. The right angles which exist around the edge of the original figure cannot act in this capacity; these have to fit together somehow inside the newly formed square.
2.   This means that the two cuts have to be at right angles to each other in order to produce the necessary four right angles.
3.   The two cuts will have to meet at a point internal to the figure in such a way as to produce no more and no less than four pieces.

These are three fairly obvious moves which could be the result of intuition rather than of any logical argument. A little more will be said about intuition later. However, writing these ideas down helps us to move on to the next stage of the problem by posing a subproblem: which points on the original shape satisfy the third criterion?

We now have to make the decision whether to work with the obvious points inside the figure, namely the corners of each small square, or to try to deal with any internal point. It would seem a reasonable strategy to keep it simple at this stage and go for the more obvious points. We could also decide at this stage to try some simpler cases (Figure 6.3).

Figure 6.3 **Simpler shapes**

There is the occasional danger that an extreme simplification, in this case reducing the problem to one square, may hide what it is we are trying to find.

If we take the simplest shape in Figure 6.3 and apply the conditions we have so far discovered, the two dissections shown in Figure 6.4 appear at first to be likely candidates. The two cuts are at right angles and they produce four pieces. Our condition to produce what look like usable right angles for the corners of the square is not met. This may or may not affect our thinking, since in order to meet this condition for this shape we have to move to a point not clearly defined inside the figure. This problem need not arise for the other shapes in Figure 6.3. How the solutions differ for each shape will become clear later.

Figure 6.4 **Attempted dissections on simple shape**

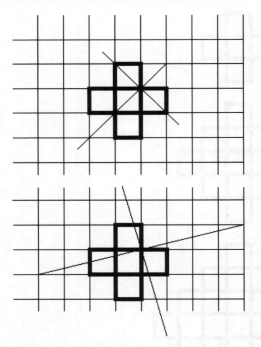

Attempts which try to make a square from the first dissection fail; we appear to be able to make only part of what seems like a larger square. From the second dissection a square of smaller proportions might be possible, but only after overlapping some of the pieces. Sooner or later we realize that we have somehow to fix the area of the square to equal the number of small squares in the original shape. So how do we do this? It appears that the angle at which the 90° cuts are placed on the original shape has some bearing on this, since one angle gives a square too big and another angle gives a square too small (Figure 6.5).

Figure 6.5 **Effect of varying cut angle: (a) square too large (b) square too small**

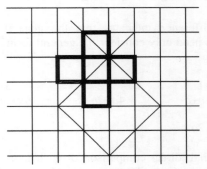

(a)

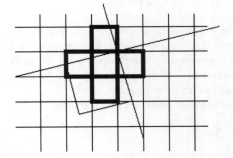

(b)

Looking for connections

We now need to count the number of small squares in the original figure. At this point the problem turns from one of geometry to one of counting and possibly algebra. Each of the following sequences represents the number of small squares in each of the original shapes. Counting by rows or columns we get:

1	1
1 + 3 + 1	5
1 + 3 + 5 + 3 + 1	13
1 + 3 + 5 + 7 + 5 + 3 + 1	25
1 + 3 + 5 + 7 + 9 + 7 + 5 + 3 + 1	41

A difference table generated from the column representing the total number of squares in each shape gives:

Number of squares:	1		5		13		25		41
First difference:		4		8		12		16	
Second differences:			4		4		4		

The constant second difference indicates that the general term is quadratic. To see this we need only consider the general form $an^2 + bn + c$ in such a table:

n	0		1		2		3
$f(n)$	c		$a+b+c$		$4a+2b+c$		$9a+3b+c$
		$a+b$		$3a+b$		$5a+b$	...
			$2a$		$2a$		

Using the leading diagonal, direct comparison of each term with the corresponding number in the first difference table gives $a = 2$, $b = 2$, $c = 1$. So now we have the following table:

n	0	1	2	3	4	. . .
No. of squares	1	5	13	25	41	. . .

The nth term, $2n^2 + 2n + 1$, is obtained by substituting these values of a, b and c in the general form $an^2 + bn + c$. This expression may hold further clues. Let us consider two alternative ways of arriving at a general term using knowledge which pupils exposed to mathematical problem-solving situations can soon acquire.

We can consider the sums of sequences of the type

$$1 + 3 + 5 + 7 + 5 + 3 + 1$$

to be twice the sum of the first n odd numbers, i.e. $2n^2$, plus the $(n+1)$th odd number, i.e. $2n+1$. So we have

$$\text{total} = 2n^2 + 2n + 1$$

Alternatively we could say that sums of sequences of this type are the sum of the first $n+1$ odd numbers, i.e. $(n+1)^2$, plus the sum of the first n odd numbers, i.e. n^2:

$$\text{total} = (n+1)^2 + n^2 = 2n^2 + 2n + 1$$

This second approach contains an expression which is rather helpful, that is $(n+1)^2 + n^2$. This expression is representative of terms of the following form:

$$2^2 + 1^2 \qquad (=5)$$
$$3^2 + 2^2 \qquad (=13)$$
$$4^2 + 3^2 \qquad (=25)$$
$$5^2 + 4^2 \qquad (=41)$$

Applying results to earlier questions

How does this relate to our original problem? Each of these expressions gives us the final piece of information we need in order to position the 90° cuts on each of the original shapes.

For the shape with 5 squares we need to satisfy the first set of conditions and provide a square of side √5 (Figure 6.6). Figure 6.6 shows four such squares superimposed on the original shape.

Figure 6.6 **Correct cut angle: square right size**

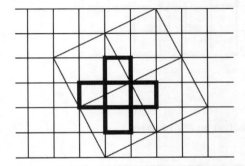

For the shape with 13 squares we need to provide a square of side √13. A simple application of Pythagoras' theorem, using the small squares as markers, enables us to simultaneously produce cuts across the original shape which are of length √13 (Figure 6.7).

Each of these figures suggests a square lattice being superimposed on to the original shape, which also gives the exact positions of each of the four pieces as they relate to the square lattice. Each of the squares can be filled by simply translating each newly formed piece parallel to the square grid lines.

Extending the problem

The question now arises: can we find other dissections by choosing a different point through which the 90° cuts pass? The shape shown in Figure 6.6 has no other point which is essentially different (except internal ones), but the shape in Figure 6.7 offers an alternative point. This produces a different dissection (Figure 6.8).

Figure 6.7 **Shape with 13 small squares: large squares of side √13**

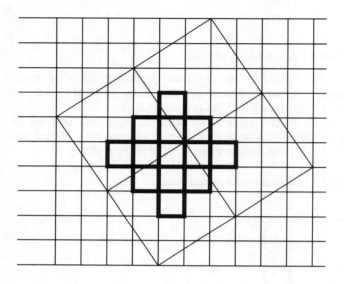

Figure 6.8 **A different dissection on the 13 shape**

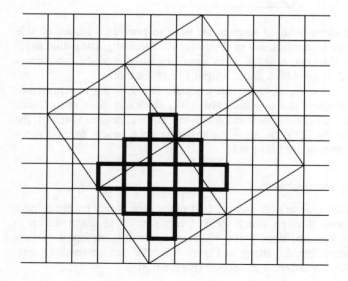

It now becomes clear that we can satisfy all the conditions without necessarily choosing an obvious point, i.e. the corner of a small square, on the original shape. Choosing any point just makes the problem of placing the 90° cuts at the correct angle a little more difficult. Clearly there are an infinite number of solutions, and we can now conjecture with some confidence that placing the 90° cuts right at the centre of the centre square will produce not only a perfect dissection but also one which comprises four congruent pieces (Figure 6.9).

Figure 6.9 **Four congruent shapes from the 13 shape**

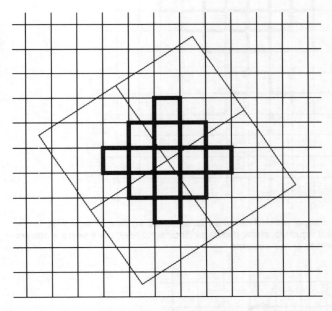

A solution to the original problem is shown in Figure 6.10.

We can investigate a little further what this situation has to offer. What happens if we make a dissection which is suitable for a square of side $\sqrt{10}$, i.e. $3^2 + 1^2$, and impose this condition on an original shape having 13 squares? Can we still make a square from the four pieces? A square of side $\sqrt{13}$ is not possible since the conditions for the corners of the square and the fitting together of pieces cannot be met. There are uncompromising gaps and overlaps. Can we make a square of side $\sqrt{10}$? If so, we would expect a net total of 3 squares to be overlapping in some way. We find that this is indeed the case (Figure 6.11).

Figure 6.10 **A solution to the original problem: 41 small squares, large square of side √41**

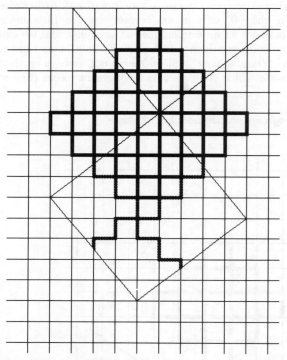

Figure 6.11 **Shape with 13 small squares, large square of side √10. Shaded small squares show overlaps (four squares), dark square shows gap: net overlap three squares**

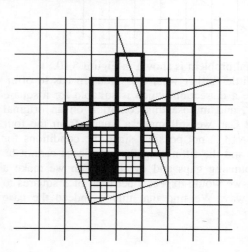

Exploring related problems

At this point we see further paths opening up for investigation. We should be able to predict the outcomes of certain dissections in the sense that a square may be formed with no gaps or overlaps; squares larger than this may be formed but will have more gaps than overlaps; and squares smaller than the perfectly fitted square may have more overlaps than gaps. Furthermore we can predict the net total area of gaps or overlaps. What is more difficult to predict is whether the original condition of having only four pieces is violated in the case of overlapping pieces. Some possibilities for exploration follow. In order to refer to a dissection easily I shall refer to a dissection to produce a square of side $\sqrt{n}$ as 'a $\sqrt{n}$ dissection', and the original shapes by the number of small squares contained therein.

1. A $\sqrt{10}$ dissection on a 13 shape will form a square with a net total of 3 unit squares overlapping (Figure 6.11).
2. A $\sqrt{10}$ dissection on a 25 shape will form a square with a net total of 15 unit squares overlapping. (Some cutting or folding of the four pieces is necessary here, and we may want to discount all such cases.)
3. A $\sqrt{8}$ dissection on a 13 shape will form a square with a net total of 5 unit squares overlapping.
4. A $\sqrt{18}$ dissection on a 13 shape will form a square with a net total of 5 unit squares missing.

The possibilities are endless, but further investigation may well reveal interesting patterns and connections. Might there be some practical application? Mathematics seems to be merging with art and design.

Proving

A question we have not really answered is whether or not we can find any other dissections *by changing the angle* at which the 90° cuts are placed with respect to the original shape. We can see from Figure 6.12 that any attempt to change the angle at which the 90° cuts are placed produces cuts across the original 13 square shape which are not $\sqrt{13}$ in length. A simple translation of each piece cannot now be made, and no other fitting seems possible.

It appears then that perfect fit solutions are only forthcoming if the angle of the 90° cuts is based upon the expression $(n+1)^2 + n^2$. We can see from Figure 6.12 that there are no integer solutions to this other than $3^2 + 2^2 = 13$, i.e. there are no other grid points which lie on the circumference of the circle of radius $\sqrt{13}$. Readers might like to satisfy themselves that the sum of two squares $(n+1)^2 + n^2$ (n integer) is a unique representation of $2n^2 + 2n + 1$ (hint: proof by contradiction).

Figure 6.12 **Changing the angle: radius √13**

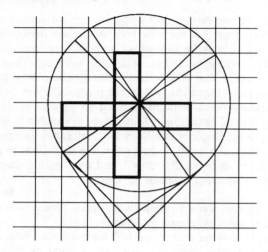

The foregoing problem is presented in the hope that some aspects of the problem-solving process are brought to life. Notice that we still do not know everything about the situation since we have chosen to extend our original problem by posing others which are closely related. This is part of the nature of investigative mathematics. A later section continues in a similar way but attempts to draw the reader's attention to the interconnectedness of certain familiar problems.

Can strategic thinking be taught?

The dissection problem has sought to illustrate problem solving in action. The outcome represents perhaps not the most elegant solution, but a solution nevertheless. It also illustrates strategic decisions which were made firstly to bring about an understanding of the problem and subsequently to develop a number of lines of attack. For example trying to come to terms with the geometry of the problem revealed another important lead. Counting the squares for special cases led to the general statement $(n+1)^2 + n^2$ which threw new light on to the geometry of the problem. This simply was not known in advance, but the connection was there, inherent in the structure of the problem, waiting to be discovered.

It would be an oversimplification to say that the strategies were sufficient to bring about an acceptable solution. The solution was produced by a human being, not a machine, so strategic thinking – planning, organizing, checking, identifying subproblems – played an important part in obtaining a solution, but only a part. Behind the strategic thinking was a person with a certain amount of belief that he might be able to solve the problem, or at least begin to understand it better. The task itself looked interesting. There was something mystifying about it, yet its structure had elements which were familiar and others not so familiar. I wanted to know how this shape could possibly fit into a square. Certainly I was motivated, and I also had the luxury of being able to choose a time of day when I could devote more than an hour to it and the time to reflect upon what I had done. I also had all the simple materials necessary to explore the situation freely: plenty of squared paper, ruler, pencil and scissors.

The main ingredients for problem solving were present:

a problem
a motivated problem solver
some strategies
enough knowledge to get started
the necessary materials to work with
time
some facility for monitoring the process.

It would seem reasonable then to suggest that successful problem solving does not come only from applying the right kind of heuristics. This may be true of problem solving by machine, but for problem solving by humans, even off-task behaviour may contribute to success. (In my case, drinking coffee and gazing out of the window.) You may well argue that we cannot allow pupils such luxuries; well, coffee perhaps not, but gazing out of the window?

I will be amongst the first to admit that the established patterns of classroom working militate against some of these important components for problem solving, but if we seriously want to improve problem-solving performance we must give more than lip service to these wider issues. Research findings indicate that strategic thinking for certain types of problem can be taught with some success (Schoenfeld 1979). Part of the secret of this success lies in emphasizing the importance of the *search* for a solution rather than the solution itself. The search holds the key to learning and enjoying mathematics. The search also holds the variation necessary to appeal to different problem solvers, to their different dispositions, learning needs and interests. The search allows connections to be made across a number of problems which seem at first sight to be quite different and unconnected. The next section illustrates how some of these connections can be made.

Variations on a theme: some simple problems

Triangles

This problem appeared a number of years ago as part of the Micro Electronics Project (MEP) Problem Solving Pack for primary schools. The problem is presented as a series of equilateral triangle patterns of the type indicated in Figure 6.13. The computer user can opt for various sizes of the large triangle by indicating the number of rows of smaller triangles to be contained therein. The problem is to find how many small triangles are contained within each specified large triangle. Although quite simple in its presentation, the problem can lead to some interesting mathematics at a number of levels in school.

Figure 6.13 **Triangle pattern**

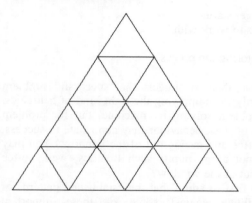

The way the problem is presented is likely to affect the kinds of strategies employed. The software in this particular instance suggests that the number of small triangles in each row should be counted and then recorded in a table. The relatively simple act of counting should not be undervalued. Counting strategy may have a significant influence upon subsequent thought patterns. Pupils may do a straight count or they may spot patterns within patterns. The first strategy results in the following table but gives little clue as to the general term for the number of triangles in each row:

Row	1	2	3	4	5 . . . n
No. of triangles per row	1	3	5	7	9 . . . $2n-1$

A second counting strategy could be to count those triangles sitting 'point upwards' and then to add the number of triangles sitting 'point downwards'. This strategy could lead to a general term being found for odd numbers by linking a visual representation of how odd numbers are formed in this case to their algebraic counterpart:

Row	1	2	3	4	5	. . .	n
No. of triangles point up	1	2	3	4	5	. . .	n
No. of triangles point down	0	1	2	3	4	. . .	$n{-}1$
No. of triangles per row	1	3	5	7	9	. . .	$2n{-}1$

In answering the final part of the problem, again the counting strategy affects the subsequent thinking. Three strategies for counting all small triangles within the large triangle are:

> a straightforward total count for each large triangle
> adding together the totals for each row, previously found
> using a points-up and points-down patterning strategy which is not restricted to rows.

A strategy which counts sequentially all small triangles within the large triangle leads to the following table:

No. of rows	1	2	3	4	5	. . .	n
No. of triangles	1	4	9	16	25	. . .	n^2

Problem solved!

The other two strategies, however, lend themselves to more investigative mathematics. Adding up the total number of triangles in each row results in the following table:

Row	1	2	3	4	5	. . .	n
No. of triangles per row	1	3	5	7	9	. . .	$2n{-}1$
Running total	1	4	9	16	25	. . .	n^2

This suggests that the sum of the first n odd numbers is n^2.

Figure 6.14 **Point-up and point-down triangles**

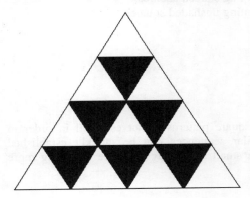

Spotting patterns of point-up triangles and point-down triangles leads to the following table:

No. of rows	1	2	3	4	5	. . .	n
No. of triangles point up	1	3	6	10	15	. . .	t_n
No. of triangles point down	0	1	3	6	10	. . .	t_{n-1}
No. of triangles	1	4	9	16	25	. . .	n^2

This suggests that $t_n + t_{n-1} = n^2$. Most readers will recognize the sequence t_n as the triangular numbers, which have a habit of turning up in unexpected places.

The first two rows of the last table suggest a further connection. The number of triangles with points up *per row* is also the row number, so

$$1 + 2 + 3 + 4 + 5 + \ . \ . \ . \ + n = t_n$$

Finding an expression for t_n in terms of n can be done geometrically, arithmetically or algebraically depending upon pupils' previous knowledge. It can be argued from the triangle patterns above, but this is far from obvious. A more obvious method is to use squares to represent unit values. In figure 6.15 the shaded squares in the left-hand diagrams represent the sequence; these are moved so that they clearly form half the original rectangle represented in the right-hand diagrams. These establish a fairly convincing pattern which suggests the generalization

$$1 + 2 + 3 + 4 + 5 + \ . \ . \ . \ + n = n(n + 1)/2$$

The arithmetic analogue to this is equally powerful. Working across the rows of the last shape in Figure 6.15 gives us

$t_4 = 1 + 2 + 3 + 4$ (counting shaded squares)
$t_4 = 4 + 3 + 2 + 1$ (counting unshaded squares)

Adding gives

$2t_4 = 5 + 5 + 5 + 5$
$2t_4 = 4 \times 5$
$t_4 = 4 \times 5/2$

Of course the link with square patterns is not essential in order to establish the result. Similar sequences can be quickly established which together are only a small step away from the following more general statements:

Figure 6.15 **Squares method for finding general expression for sequence**

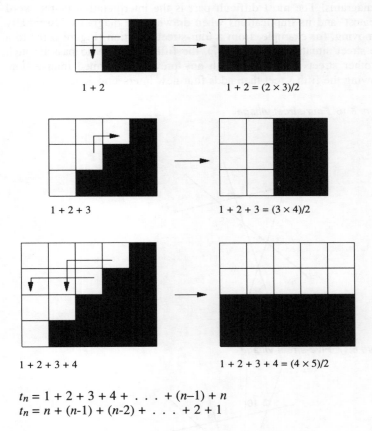

$1 + 2$

$1 + 2 = (2 \times 3)/2$

$1 + 2 + 3$

$1 + 2 + 3 = (3 \times 4)/2$

$1 + 2 + 3 + 4$

$1 + 2 + 3 + 4 = (4 \times 5)/2$

$$t_n = 1 + 2 + 3 + 4 + \ldots + (n-1) + n$$
$$t_n = n + (n-1) + (n-2) + \ldots + 2 + 1$$

These give

$$2t_n = (n+1) + (n+1) + (n+1) + \ldots + (n+1) \ (n \text{ times})$$
$$t_n = n(n+1)/2$$

Village streets

In a village there are three streets. All the streets are straight. One lamp-post is put up at each crossroads. What is the greatest number of lamp-posts that could be needed? Now try four streets and five streets. Predict the answer for six streets, then check it. Can you see a pattern? Why does the pattern work? (Burton 1984:78)

Here again there are straightforward links between the visual representation of the problem and a numerical one. The problem, set out in this way, leads pupils into the problem area through the drawing of diagrams. The most difficult part is the interpretation of the word 'greatest' and its implications when drawing the diagrams. Essentially in moving, for example, from a four-street situation (Figure 6.16) to a five-street situation (Figure 6.17), the fifth street has to pass through all other streets but not through any previously formed intersection. Drawing the fifth street then adds four new intersections.

Figure 6.16 **Four-street village**

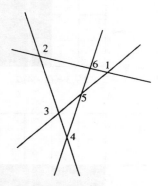

Figure 6.17 **Five-street village**

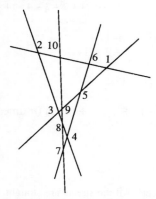

So drawing the *n*th street adds *n*-1 intersections. This is similar to adding the *n*th row of triangles in the previous problem, which adds *n*–1 point-down triangles. It is not surprising then that the triangular numbers appear again:

No. of streets (*s*)   1   2   3   4   5 . . . *s*
No. of posts (*p*)   0   1   3   6   10 . . . *s*(*s*–1)/2

A number of extensions to the problem are possible. One such extension is that each new street should now be perpendicular to the previous one. The increases in the number of intersections (posts) now occur in constant pairs, leading to a less obvious sequence:

No. of streets (*s*)   1   2   3   4   5   6   7   8   9   10 . . .
No. of posts (*p*)   0   1   2   4   6   9   12   16   20   25 . . .

However, inspection of the sequence for an even number of streets reveals the familiar squares sequence, and for an odd number of streets shows twice the triangular number sequence. It is left to the reader to establish or verify that $p(s\ \text{even}) = s^2/4$ and $p(s\ \text{odd}) = (s^2 - 1)/4$.

Diagonals

Essentially the problem states: 'Draw four dots on a circle. Join them up. Choose one point only and see how many diagonals you can draw in from it.' Try the same thing with five points, six points and so on. (Burton 1984:122)

Once pupils have the meaning of 'diagonal' clear, the problem becomes a simple matter of recording the number of diagonals (any straight line joining two non-adjacent points) for a given number of points on the circle. For fairly obvious reasons to us the number of diagonals is three less than the number of points (Figure 6.18), so the mapping is

n (number of points) → (*n*–3) (number of diagonals)

for integer *n*≥3.

Figure 6.18 **Two diagonals from point A**

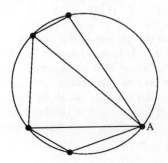

If we draw in all diagonals from all points (Figure 6.19) then, allowing for the fact that each diagonal will be drawn twice, the number of diagonals will be $n(n-3)/2$. If we also count the two chords which can be drawn from each point, the results can be extended down to $n = 1$, and we discover the triangular numbers yet again:

No. of points	1	2	3	4	5	6	. . .	n
No. of lines	0	1	3	6	10	15	. . .	$n(n-1)/2$

Figure 6.19 **Four lines joining each point to every other point**

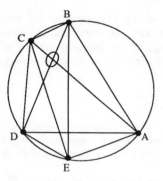

However, the link with the triangular numbers may be argued from the result for the number of diagonals $n(n-3)/2$. By including the two chords from each point, the number of lines joining each point to every other point is $n-1$. So for n points, there will be $n(n-1)/2$ lines.

It is possible that pupils who are encouraged to ask their own questions or modify problems may suggest counting the number of intersections as well. This is a more demanding exercise because the number of intersections increases rapidly and counting errors may creep in. The resulting table is difficult to generalize.

No. of points	1	2	3	4	5	6	7	8	. . .	n
No. of intersections	0	0	0	1	5	15	35	70	. . .	

Readers may recognize this as one of the diagonal columns of Pascal's triangle (see Figure 6.23). It is the diagonal labelled $^nC_4$. Can this be reasoned out from the situations as presented by Figure 6.19? By focusing our attention on one intersection only (marked with a circle) we can see that it is determined uniquely by the four points A, B, C, D. Every other point of intersection is similarly determined – any four points from n points will suffice – so the number of intersections is $^nC_4$, or equivalently

$$(n^4 - 6n^3 + 11n^2 - 6n)/24$$

I shall come back to this result in a moment.

Before leaving the easier problem, readers may also like to look at the last but one table in relation to the 'handshakes' problem or the 'mystic rose' problem as it appears in the Shell/JMB pack 'Problems with Patterns and Numbers'. The table is repeated here:

No. of points	1	2	3	4	5	6	. . .	n
No. of lines	0	1	3	6	10	15	. . .	$n(n-1)/2$

The 'handshakes' or 'tournament' problem has become a popular one in secondary classrooms recently. It simply asks: 'If there are 20 people at a party and each person shakes hands with every other person exactly once, how many handshakes will take place?' It has been used very successfully to initiate discussions within small groups of pupils. Its popularity may also be due to the fact that a number of routes to a solution can be found by pupils and that pupils easily relate to the problem of counting the number of different handshakes possible between a given number of people.

'Find the number of different lines determined by n points, where no three points are collinear' is essentially the same problem but would no doubt get a different reception from pupils. The 'handshakes' problem may well evoke a number of different responses, but can be rather limiting for other kinds of development with pupils of high ability. For example, the problem stated in a more abstract form lends itself to more abstract development: 'How many different planes are determined by n points, where no three points are collinear and no four points are coplanar?' It is difficult to see how this could be asked from a 'handshakes' perspective.

Posing a problem extension as succinctly as this by pupils is unlikely for a first attempt. Interpreting the implications of working in three dimensions can challenge the most able pupil, and an extra condition like 'no four points being coplanar' is more likely to come after considerable thought and discussion. Three points soon emerge as the minimum number of points required to determine a plane. The addition of another point, not coplanar with the other three, soon reveals that three further planes can be determined. For example, consider the vertices A, B, C, D of the tetrahedron shown in Figure 6.20 as being four such points.

The addition of another point, no four being coplanar, reveals ten planes (Figure 6.21), five planes being determined by the five 'small' triangles ABC, BCD, CDE, ADE, ABE and another five planes by the five 'large' triangles ACE, ABD, BCE, ACD, BDE. The addition of more points makes drawing less profitable. However, Figure 6.21 together with the knowledge that no three points are collinear and no four points coplanar indicates that the problem can be reduced to one of asking: 'How many ways can we select three different points from

Figure 6.20 **Four non-coplanar points determining $^4C_3$ planes**

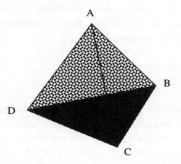

Figure 6.21 **Five points, no four being coplanar, determining $^5C_3$ planes**

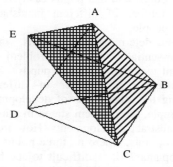

Figure 6.22 **Five points, no four being coplanar, determining $^5C_4$ three-dimensional shapes: one of the five tetrahedra BCDE is shown**

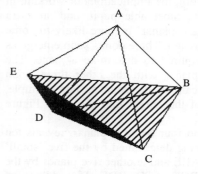

five given points?' The problem remains principally a counting problem and one which increases in complexity as each extra point is added. Without the knowledge of ^nC_r notation and how it fits into this context, counting would have to be very methodical in order to account for the occurrence of each plane. This example illustrates the power which mathematics has to short-circuit a problem situation, but first a problem isomorph had to be identified before the mathematics became meaningful. The power of mathematics is also demonstrated by the fact that we can now go on with some confidence to ask whether the same thinking will count the number of three-dimensional figures determined by n points ($n \geq 4$) (Figure 6.22).

The results of this thinking can be summarized as follows:

1. The number of lines determined by n points ($n \geq 2$) is $^nC_2$.
2. The number of planes determined by n points ($n \geq 3$) is $^nC_3$
3. The number of three-dimensional shapes determined by n points ($n \geq 4$) is $^nC_4$.

This pattern extends to higher dimensions and thinking becomes more abstract, but for those who wish to pursue the pattern, consider Pascal's triangle (Figure 6.23) and how this may relate to the above solutions.

Figure 6.23 **Pascal's triangle**

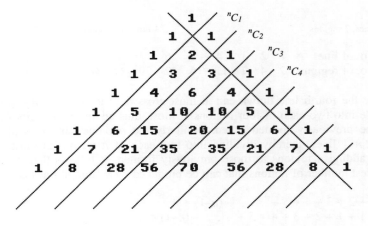

A similar kind of thinking can be evoked by asking: 'What is the greatest number of regions into which the plane can be divided by n straight lines?' Again, grasping that 'greatest' means no two lines can be parallel and no three lines can be concurrent is a crucial first understanding of the problem. The second important point is that in satisfying only these conditions there is no loss of generality in the sense that the result is independent of the different configurations possible. So we have (Figure 6.24):

Figure 6.24 **Division of plane**

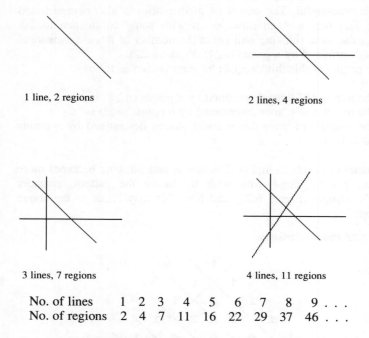

1 line, 2 regions

2 lines, 4 regions

3 lines, 7 regions

4 lines, 11 regions

No. of lines	1	2	3	4	5	6	7	8	9 . . .
No. of regions	2	4	7	11	16	22	29	37	46 . . .

Since the fourth line drawn can at most cross only three lines, it can divide into two each of four regions at most, thus adding four regions to the previously formed seven. Similarly the nth line can cross at most $n-1$ lines, thereby dividing into two each of n regions at most, thus adding n regions to those previously formed. It follows that the greatest number of regions that can be produced by n straight lines is

$$2 + 2 + 3 + 4 + 5 + \ldots + (n-1) + n$$
$$= 1 + 1 + 2 + 3 + 4 + 5 + \ldots + (n-1) + n$$
$$= 1 + n(n-1)/2 + n$$
$$= 1 + n + {}^nC_2$$

Can we arrive at this result by a different route? The argument seems to involve the number of times the last line drawn crosses all previously drawn lines, i.e. the number of intersections. What happens if we count these instead? (Note that we have already done this in the 'village streets' problem.) Consideration of the diagrams in Figure 6.25 soon leads to the conjecture

$$\text{no. of regions} = 1 + \text{no. of lines} + \text{no. of intersections}$$
$$= 1 + n + {}^nC_2$$

Figure 6.25 **Division of plane showing intersections**

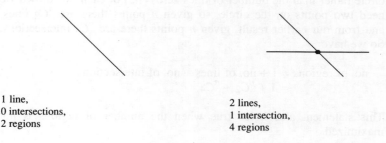

1 line,
0 intersections,
2 regions

2 lines,
1 intersection,
4 regions

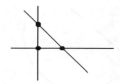

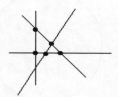

3 lines,
3 intersections,
7 regions

4 lines,
6 intersections,
11 regions

There is another interesting connection we can make with what is generally regarded as a more difficult problem, and one which is often used as a warning against arriving at a premature conclusion about patterns in number sequences. The problem is to relate the number of regions formed within the circle to the points on its circumference. The regions are formed by joining each point to every other point (Figure 6.26):

No. of points (n)   1   2   3   4   5 . . .
No. of regions   1   2   4   8   16 . . .

This is very strong evidence which suggests that

no. of regions $= 2^{n-1}$ (n is number of points)

However, careful counting of the regions in Figure 6.26 shows that the number of regions for six points is 31. Most pupils will believe they are missing a region somewhere in their counting. A look at the related problems soon reveals that 31 is correct. We can apply the same principles for counting regions; nothing really has changed except that we are now trying to relate to regions the number of points around a circle rather than the number of lines across it. For each line drawn we need two points on the circle, so given n points there are $^nC_2$ lines; and from our earlier result, given n points there are $^nC_4$ intersections. So we have

no. of regions = 1 + no. of lines + no. of intersections
$$= 1 + {}^nC_2 + {}^nC_4$$

This statement also holds true when the number of regions is not maximized.

Figure 6.26 **Relationships between regions in a circle and points on its circumference**

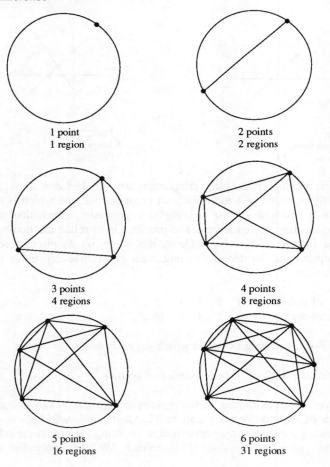

1 point
1 region

2 points
2 regions

3 points
4 regions

4 points
8 regions

5 points
16 regions

6 points
31 regions

Organising for problem solving

Anyone contemplating using a problem-solving approach or increasing time spent on problem solving will need to have some idea of the kinds of teaching strategies they can employ. In order to have a satisfactory problem-solving programme it is essential that you have access to a variety of problems. This seems self-evident, but without a good working knowledge of problem types, their difficulty, and the kinds of problem-solving strategies which can bring success, one is unlikely to design and operate a satisfactory problem-solving programme.

All the problem types considered in this chapter can be labelled process problems, so called since the emphasis lies in the process of finding a solution, perhaps one solution amongst many. During this process the pupil will need to find an appropriate strategy or strategies. As already indicated, strategies form an important link between solver and solution (Figure 6.27).

Figure 6.27 **Strategies in problem solving**

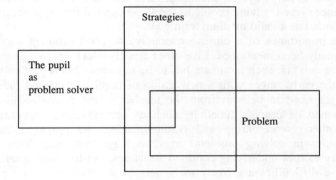

Clearly part of the teacher's task is to find a suitable match between the strategies known to be useful in solving a problem and the strategies that are known to a particular pupil or group of pupils. Without this important link no problem-solving programme will be successful. Again this emphasizes the need for the teacher to be an active problem solver, since it is through first-hand experience of solving *unfamiliar* problems that appropriate strategies can be best identified. The post-Cockcroft era has seen much more support for teachers in this regard, but the choosing of problems for a programme should be based on some knowledge about the problem area ideally gained from first-hand experience of attempting a solution. Support of this nature, for example suggesting which types of problem are suitable for certain ability ranges, ought to be viewed only as suggestions and should not be taken at face value. There can be no substitute for individual teachers seeking out appropriate problems for the pupils in their care. Appropriate problem presentation and adaptation is again best done by the teacher who has a detailed knowledge of both problem and pupil.

Research as reported by Suydam (1980:36) has pointed to a number of characteristics which good problem solvers possess and suggests a matching number of teaching points which can be used to develop these abilities. These teaching points tend to be rather general and will require some individual interpretation in order to be effective. For example, in order to develop an ability in pupils to recognize a sameness or a difference or an analogy across problems it is suggested that pupils should have experience of classifying problems. This presupposes that the pupils have already solved a number of similar problems or have the ability to extrapolate some common structural features from a number of situations. Those who can do this are probably already quite good problem solvers. Those who are not able to do this will not acquire this facility overnight. Such intuition feeds on experience, and the types of experiences which develop insight are often hard to come by. To encourage reflection on the similarities and differences when solving problems, however limited this may be, must be regarded as a valid medium term goal.

The importance of a climate conducive to good problem solving has already been mentioned. Like other aspects which encourage good problem solving, such a climate has to be nurtured; this is particularly so in the early stages with a new group of pupils. Overt and hidden messages need to be sent from the teacher to the pupils about the importance of process functions such as perseverance, cooperation with others, representing and communicating the problem. Early difficulties in solving problems may, as suggested, stem from the inability to spot underlying common structures, but the manifestations of these difficulties are likely to be related to affective as much as cognitive factors (see for example Silver 1985).

Inexperienced problem solvers will show a number of emotions as they try to come to terms with an unfamiliar problem, even if appropriate strategies and content area lie within the experience of the solver. Part of the risk lies in providing enough challenge without causing undue tension, lack of progress and frustration. The challenge for teachers is in strengthening the problem-solving base so that more challenging problems may be presented without a corresponding reduction in successes. The very nature of problem solving demands that we should give our attention to such affective issues. When an unfamiliar problem is first met, pupils should be made aware that seeing a solution immediately or choosing a correct method to a solution first time is not expected of them. It is at this early stage of problem solving that emotions are likely to run at their highest, and unless pupils are given support these will develop into negative responses. If pupils have been used to the 'quick fix' type of mathematics then a sudden blockage to their progress often leads to an abandoning of any attempt at a solution. However, a climate could exist in which pupils expect to have difficulties as part of the problem-solving process, and so, in meeting an initial blockage, alternative strategies for dealing with it can be found. This demands a greater awareness on the part of pupils of their own mental processes and emotional states. A growing awareness in these directions may lead to greater stamina in coping with the fluctuating emotions associated with being stuck, finding a way, only to become stuck again. It may be that more progress can be made in problem solving by paying more attention to pupils' metacognitive and organizational processes and how their emotional states relate to these processes as well as to the cognitive aspects. A classroom climate in which positive attitudes prevail may provide the necessary stable background against which the energies generated by these emotions may be successfully directed.

Much of what was said in Chapter 4 on enriching the process of learning applies directly to a problem-solving context. Chapter 4 concentrates on mapping out purposeful activity and on how the teacher's knowledge of content, related activities and pupil behaviour could be used to enhance learning. Teaching for problem solving demands all these skills and more.

Before leaving the subject of problem solving, a summary of some of the important points for developing a problem-solving approach might prove useful:

1. Choose appropriate problems based on your knowledge of
   (a) the content of the problems
   (b) the strategies for their solution
   (c) pupils' problem-solving skills.
2. Decide how problems will be tackled:
   (a) individually
   (b) in pairs
   (c) in larger groups.
3. Decisions made in 1 and 2 will affect how you want to present problems and will determine the type and quantity of materials required.
4. Problems can encourage convergent thinking and focus on specific skills, or may encourage divergent thinking, creativity and intuition.
5. Anticipate early difficulties in getting started and plan helping questions and helping strategies which do not take away pupils' initiatives.

6. Allow enough time for problems to be understood and debated. Develop key questions aimed at exposing the level of pupils' understanding.
7. Listen to pupils' ideas without responding in an evaluative way. Expect the unexpected.
8. Accept the pupils' right to be wrong.
9. Encourage discussion between pupils by reducing your own input.
10. Encourage different levels of communication appropriate to the following problem-solving stages:
    (a) exploratory stage
    (b) reflecting stage
    (c) reporting stage.
11. Plan for reflecting on problems, extending problems and connecting with other familiar problems.

Further reading

Gardiner A. 1987(b) *Mathematical Puzzling* Oxford University Press
Holding J. 1991 *The investigations book* Cambridge University Press
Mason J. 1985 *Thinking Mathematically* Addison-Wesley
Wells D. 1988 *Hidden Connections, Double Meanings* Cambridge University Press

CHAPTER 7

Mathematics and turtle geometry

Chapter 4 seeks to identify themes and interconnections which enrich the process of learning. Chapter 6 focuses on the processes of mathematical problem solving and its teaching. Many regard using turtle geometry, available now on microcomputers, as a natural step forward in bringing together problems or ideas which are mathematically rich in content and the relatively novel processes by which these problems may be solved. This chapter considers some of the possibilities which Logo offers mathematics learning and teaching, and indicates some possible dangers which enthusiasts need to be aware of. For the first part of this chapter some basic knowledge of Logo is assumed and access to a widely available version of Logo on a microcomputer will help as you read through the chapter. The second part of the chapter assumes rather more knowledge of the Logo language.

The turtle is a computer controlled robot which is floor or screen based. Simple computer commands can be given which drive the robot forwards or backwards or which turn the robot through a given angle. The attraction of its use is that even very young children can relate to its movement by drawing on their own body knowledge.

Logo and turtle programming

The Logo language, which supports a turtle geometry environment, was developed as long ago as 1968 by artificial intelligence researchers attempting to understand and simulate human thinking processes. The most well known of these researchers is Seymour Papert, whose book *Mindstorms* (1980) describes the power of Logo not only for mathematics learning and thinking but also for learning about learning and thinking about thinking. The teaching of mathematical ideas through computer programming was to become one of the main foci of development for Logo enthusiasts throughout the 1970s. The driving principle behind the development, no doubt influenced by Papert's association with Piaget, was that given the right environment or culture children could 'learn without being taught'. Logo was designed in order to provide such an environment where children could learn by discovery and experience in much the same way as children naturally learn the language of their mother tongue. In describing his own book Papert says that it is a book 'about how culture, a way of thinking, an idea comes to inhabit a young mind' (p. 10). Papert goes on to describe the turtle as an object 'to think with' but observes that there may be better turtles 'yet to be invented'. However, the basic screen turtle (a pointer in the shape of a small triangle) driven by simple commands entered via a keyboard provides a necessary action, expounded by Piaget, required for the development of mental operations.

Logo became available on microcomputers in Britain by 1984, although a version was used in Edinburgh as early as 1979. Subsequently a number of versions of Logo became available, but the four fundamental commands FORWARD, BACKWARD, RIGHT and LEFT are common to all and provide the basis for the 'computational style of geometry' as perceived by Papert. The simplicity in using such commands makes this new style of geometry available to even very young children. Whether a floor turtle or a screen-based turtle is used, the effects of using these commands can be seen immediately even if not fully understood. The two concepts 'distance' and 'angle' are experienced as direct outcomes or outputs of simple program commands. The concept of distance as conveyed by the turtle presents few difficulties, but the concept of angle in a turtle environment is more problematic. The floor turtle relates more directly to the experience of the young child since the floor turtle's action takes place in a horizontal plane, and rotations rather than angles are more obviously related to LEFT and RIGHT commands. The movement of the floor turtle is relatively slow but its movement alone is sufficient to stimulate young minds without the need to draw lines as it moves. The normal screen turtle on the other hand moves quickly and it is relatively uninteresting unless lines are drawn indicating the route it has just travelled. Rotations are much less obvious; they take place in a vertical plane and initially can be confusing for the novice user. There are other difficulties associated with the concept of angle which will be discussed in a moment.

Some of the claims made for using Logo, such as the improved ability to monitor one's own thinking processes, are supported by empirical research findings; others, such as transfer or the generalizability of skills and the development of concepts, are proving more difficult to substantiate (Krasnor and Mitterer 1984; Clements and Gullo 1984; de Corte and Verschaffel 1986). Krasnor and Mitterer (1984) point out what are perceived to be the 'powerful ideas' to which Papert refers. These are the processes by which problems are solved and in essence are no different from the processes described in Chapter 6. In particular they list the following: to be able to break down problems into manageable subproblems; to be systematic in planning to achieve goals; to be able to successively refine program solutions through the process of debugging; and to develop a positive attitude to making errors. They go on to point out that 'there is as yet no good evidence that any of the powerful ideas mentioned above generalize to other domains' (p. 137). There is however such a sufficiency of interest and enthusiasm for Logo that conditions for its effective use are urgently required. Early evidence suggests that much was expected of Logo, for example that the richness inherent in its use would be sufficient to promote general problem-solving skills to a level where they could be transferable to other situations. The motivating effect of using Logo is in no doubt and it is in the affective domain that most gains are perceived to be made. Before considering further what research may have to tell us about using Logo with children, let us look at some possibilities for its use in order to identify where the claims for children's learning may lie.

Consider for the moment, from both a mathematical point of view and a programming point of view, one of the simplest situations that turtle geometry via a screen turtle can present. The instructions

FORWARD 70
RIGHT 45
FORWARD 60

result in a picture being drawn as shown in Figure 7.1. It is quite clear which path the turtle has taken from its starting position at A to its final position at C, i.e. the child sees the total effect of his/her program. However, if we consider intermediate snapshots of this complex event (in the sense of more than a single action taking place) a number of remarks may be made (see Figure 7.2).

Figure 7.1 **Simple turtle path**

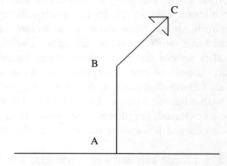

The first command FORWARD 70 changes the turtle's *position state*; the second command changes the turtle's *heading state* (from zero); and the third command changes the turtle's position state again. The visual effect of this is that the turtle produces what most children

Figure 7.2 **Breakdown of simple turtle path**

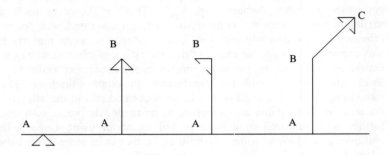

would perceive to be an angle. Visually BC is connected to AB at B (i.e. two lines meeting at a point) and their relative positions are distinguished by the *visible* angle which lies between them and its defining point at B, in this case 135°. The program coding indicates that its effect at B is the result of the command RIGHT 45, a command which changes the turtle's heading state. This is a transitory change, the result of which is made permanent only by changing the turtle's position state which indicates in a *coded form* the change in the heading state which has taken place at B.

The ease with which Logo can be used to create intricate figures and the speed with which the screen turtle changes its heading are factors which have encouraged Logo enthusiasts to overlook this possible source of confusion for novice users. For an indication of how profound this confusion is in 9- and 10-year-olds see Simmons and Cope (1990) and Cope and Simmons (1991). Any diagnosis of this confusion is difficult in a normal turtle geometry environment where there are many factors which interact. One of the early manifestations of this confusion is when pupils move from drawing a square, a typical starting point, to drawing an equilateral triangle. Earlier experiences of geometry whether school based or environment based naturally engage a visual, static aspect of our perceptions; we view a triangle (equilateral or not) as having three, often fixed points, and each of these points together with adjacent sides as forming three fixed interior angles. Any reference to external, supplementary angles is not necessary and may even be considered somewhat bizarre (see Figure 7.3).

This is plainly not the case in a turtle geometry environment; some knowledge, whether procedurally based or conceptually based, linking program commands which change the turtle's heading state to what has just happened and to what is conjectured will happen next is a fundamental requirement for the *sound* development of mathematical and programming concepts.

Figure 7.3 **Equilateral triangle with external angles**

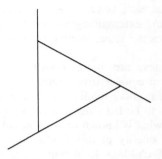

Novice programmers, typically aged 8 to 11 years, attempting to draw an equilateral triangle without the necessary background knowledge find it difficult to move from what is known – that an equilateral triangle has interior angles of 60° – to the required turtle rotation of 120° at each vertex. Incremental, trial and error attempts at finding the correct angle tend to dominate the problem-solving activity and the accumulative effect of combinations of LEFT and RIGHT commands is lost. Deductive reasoning based upon geometrical considerations of supplementary angles or equal divisions of the 'total turtle trip' of 360° is not induced merely through Logo activity. (In describing any simple closed curve, i.e. where no part of the curve crosses any other part, the turtle will turn a total of 360°. If the curve is allowed to cross itself, the total turn may be an integral multiple of 360°.) Teacher awareness of this problem and subsequent intervention of an explanatory type have little effect on outcomes if the children concerned have not yet reached the necessary stage of awareness (Cope *et al.* 1992). It appears then that part of the solution to this problem lies in raising pupils' awareness of the properties connected with turtle graphics.

Part of this awareness raising would seem, as before, to lie in the direction of finding situations which challenge pupils' possible misconceptions and then supporting their problem-solving activities in constructive ways as discussed in Chapter 6. For example in Chapter 6 part of the problem-solving skills repertoire was the ability to identify a sameness which may exist across apparently different problems. As Papert (1980:75) points out, a sameness does exist across the two problems of drawing a square and drawing an equilateral triangle in Logo. The sameness appeals to the body knowledge referred to earlier whereby 'walking round' the perimeter of each closed shape results in the same amount of turn. Why this is thought to be observable *before* the task is completed is not clear, and it would appear necessary for children to have many hours of exploratory Logo and other body knowledge experiences before becoming aware that this might be true.

Another sameness has to be invoked: that both the square and the equilateral triangle are regular figures which, in a turtle environment, translate to 'the turtle rotation at each vertex is an equal division of 360°'. Hence for n equal sides and external angles, and external angle a, we have $na = 360°$. This gives the required rotation at each vertex as $a = 360°/n$.

These ideas, as Papert states, are more powerful and more generalizable than their Euclidean counterparts – and, *given sufficient exposure* to the Logo environment, more intelligible. The power to be gained from using Logo appears to be from the relatively easy way in which children can move from what is known to what is unknown by interacting with the turtle. The quality of this interaction is at least dependent upon the ability of children to debug program errors, recognize similarities in program structures and apply some level of reasoning to the process. The square and triangle problems are sufficient as examples of how this might happen. Initial attempts at drawing squares and triangles usually follow a pattern of repeating commands where the approach is at a visual level in the sense that the effect of each command is seen before the next command is given. These early programs will take a form similar to the following:

Triangle	*Square*
FORWARD 55	FORWARD 55
RIGHT 120	RIGHT 90
FORWARD 55	FORWARD 55
RIGHT 120	RIGHT 90
FORWARD 55	FORWARD 55
RIGHT 120	RIGHT 90
	FORWARD 55
	RIGHT 90

In this 'visual effects' mode the last command is often not given since the shape is complete even though the total rotation is not 360°. Only in looking for completeness, either in a full turn of the turtle or in the patterns emerging from the coding, will this final instruction seem necessary. This is a first step towards recognizing the program structure common to both tasks. It would seem appropriate at this stage to ask children to speculate what they would see as the coding for a regular five-sided figure. The solution may result from trial and error attempts at a 'visual effects' level, or from reasoned argument based upon a recognized commonality between the first two solutions. The realization that $5 \times 72° = 360°$, and a repeat of the pair of instructions FORWARD and RIGHT five times, would be an exemplification of how aspects of formal geometry and turtle geometry were being linked and were made accessible through the Logo language.

The coding above, to the experienced eye, almost begs the use of the facility provided by the REPEAT construct:

REPEAT 4[FORWARD 55 RIGHT 90] (square)
REPEAT 5[FORWARD 55 RIGHT 72] (regular pentagon)

However, recent research has shown that connections such as these are not automatically made by pupils simply by exposing them to Logo (de Corte and Verschaffel 1989; Hoyles and Sutherland 1989:183). This is not an implied call for teacher intervention on a scale which removes those inherent and very desirable aspects of learning mathematics through using Logo; however, there is now a general acceptance that teaching towards specific learning outcomes is necessary even within a Logo environment. An example of this here would be to assist pupils to make the necessary links towards a more general statement leading to the use of the REPEAT construct. A step towards a generalization would be to write 360/5 for the parameter of the RIGHT command. This could be based on an inductive pattern connecting external angles with a total turn of 360° and/or from geometrical considerations. The following pattern then emerges:

REPEAT 3[FORWARD 55 RIGHT 360/3] (equilateral triangle)
REPEAT 4[FORWARD 55 RIGHT 360/4] (square)
REPEAT 5[FORWARD 55 RIGHT 360/5] (regular pentagon)
. . .
REPEAT n[FORWARD 55 RIGHT 360/n] (regular *n*-gon)

However, the use of the last REPEAT command would require an appreciation of the role of variable in Logo.

The description of the turtle 'as an object to think with' implies that its usefulness in learning situations is wider than the rather obvious connections with geometry. The role of turtle geometry in developing algebraic thinking is of the same vintage as its role for developing spatial thinking. The facility afforded by the Logo language to introduce the use of variable in a semi-formal way through programming by completing a relatively simple drawing task is a major contributor to the 'powerful ideas' referred to by Papert. For example, any task which asks for a simple shape to be drawn to a certain size will require some understanding of the geometry of the shape and the respective lengths involved. To then ask for the size to be changed may stimulate the need to introduce a variable into the program. (For a full discussion of variable in Logo see Noss and Hoyles 1987; Sutherland 1989.)

A suitable vehicle for introducing the idea of variable is the use of procedures. This is the facility within Logo to name a piece of code which can then be referred to by that name. For example, using the REPEAT command above, a procedure for drawing an equilateral triangle in Logo would be as follows:

```
TO TRI
REPEAT 3[FORWARD 55 RIGHT 360/3]
```

A call of TRI would then be sufficient to draw an equilateral triangle of side length 55 units. By asking pupils to change the size of the triangle we would then focus their attention on the content of the REPEAT command and encourage them to discriminate between the FORWARD and RIGHT commands. If pupils understand how the triangle is drawn then they will quickly conclude that the 55 referred to by the FORWARD command is the number to change. Observations of children working with Logo confirm the expectation that children will be happy to keep changing the number of FORWARD units to achieve the desired effect, but at least by doing this they experience using different numbers to achieve different effects.

It is believed that exposure to this kind of work will make the idea of variable more meaningful than many of the symbolic representations to be found in formal algebra. Certainly understanding that a variable can represent a range of numbers in a Logo context seems a smaller step to make than the conceptual leaps that have to be made when trying to understand what expressions of the type $x+2$ might mean. The use of mnemonic names for variables also helps understanding, but it should be realized that variables may be defined by any letter string including a single letter. Thus the procedure

```
TO TRI :SIDE
REPEAT 3[FORWARD :SIDE RIGHT 360/3]
```

is a first step towards a more general procedure.

It may be useful at this point to reflect upon some of the categories used by Sutherland (1989) in her recent research. The categories provided 'a framework for analysing pupil understanding' for the use of variable in a Logo context and in a more formal algebraic context. They are (p. 323):

1. Acceptance of the idea of variable (deemed present if pupils did not reject the use of variable).
2. Understanding that a variable name represents a range of numbers.
3. Understanding that any variable name can be used.
4. Understanding that different variable names can represent the same value.
5. Acceptance of 'lack of closure' in a variable dependent expression.
6. Understanding of the nature of the second-order relationship between two variable dependent expressions.
7. Ability to use variable to represent a general method.

Confident use of the above TRI procedure with a parameter SIDE would indicate that pupils had accepted the idea of using variables and that a variable name can represent a range of numbers. There may be understanding as defined by categories 3 and 4 but this could not be diagnosed from the use of this simple procedure. Additionally seven categories of use of variables were identified (p. 324):

(a) One variable input to a procedure.
(b) Variable as scale factor.
(c) More than one variable input to a procedure.
(d) Variable operated on within a procedure.
(e) Variable input to define a mathematical function in Logo.
(f) General superprocedure.
(g) Recursive procedure.

In our case TRI invokes category (a). Category (b), the idea of scale factor, is not strictly invoked by the second version of TRI. However, since pupils often work from fixed procedures, like the first version of TRI, it may be that their understanding of variable manifests itself as

```
TO TRI :SIDE
REPEAT 3[FORWARD 55 * :SIDE RIGHT 360/3]
```

Here :SIDE has lost its mnemonic quality but acts now as a scale factor for the sides of the triangle to produce mathematically similar triangles. New developments can be explored by linking the inputs of this new procedure to the inputs of the previous one. For example:

```
TRI 55 ↔ TRI 1
TRI 110 ↔ TRI 2
TRI 22 ↔ TRI ?
TRI ? ↔ TRI −1
```

Here procedure calls invoking the scale factor approach are on the right.

We can now return to our first attempt at using a REPEAT construct which uses a variable in order to produce a regular *n*-gon:

```
REPEAT :N[FORWARD 55 RIGHT 360/:N]
```

Our TRI procedure changes to:

```
TO POLY :SIDE :N
REPEAT :N[FORWARD :SIDE RIGHT 360/:N]
```

The two inputs now allow for a change in side length and a change in the number of sides. This is the POLY1 procedure referred to in Chapter 2.

Logo procedures then, amongst other things, are powerful devices for introducing algebraic ideas through a process of development which allows pupils to see the effects of their various uses. It should be noted that this rather sketchy introduction to the various aspects of variable in Logo would not be an adequate introduction to variable from a pupil point of view. Many hours of Logo experience appear to be necessary for children to become fully conversant with these aspects, and we should not assume that mere exposure to problem solving using Logo will be sufficient in itself either to improve programming skills or to instil the general ability to solve mathematically related problems.

Nonetheless Logo does provide yet another avenue for developing mathematical thinking, programming skills and strategies for problem solving. This lies in the ease with which Logo procedures, with or without parameters, can act as building blocks to produce more complex procedures; or conversely, how a complex problem may be made more manageable by breaking down the problem into subproblems (subprocedures) which can be dealt with more easily at a mathematical or programming level.

As I have already indicated, much of the present criticism of current use of programming to enhance mathematical thinking skills lies in the fact that it is too easy for pupils to attempt new solutions by changing, with little thought, different aspects of their program. Most of us recognize that there are some benefits to be gained by this kind of approach, but such activity tends to stay at a very superficial level and inhibits rather than enhances mathematical thinking skills. The teacher's role in encouraging the latter remains as vital when using Logo as with any other teaching medium. The questioning skills and organizing for discussions developed in previous chapters apply here and the use of pencil and paper away from a computer should be encouraged. Some of these points can be illustrated by suggesting a series of related turtle tasks.

Turtle tasks for development

Consider the POLY procedure as a starting point:

```
TO POLY :SIDE :N
REPEAT :N[FORWARD :SIDE RIGHT 360/:N]
```

Embedded in this procedure is the knowledge that the number of sides N is related to the external angle A by the equation $A = 360/N$. Ways and means of raising awareness about this knowledge are of course not restricted to the Logo environment, and the teacher's role as questioner and mentor combined with effective feedback from the computer can be a powerful force for learning. In this case a number of mathematically related tasks and questions can be posed in order to develop pupils' awareness of the mathematics of this situation and to develop their thinking into other situations. The ideas are presented as a series of possible questions and tasks to be completed; it is left to the reader to find an appropriate way of implementing them to fit individual circumstances.

1. Call the POLY procedure with different (integer) values of N, keeping the side length the same. A small side length may be necessary to keep the whole drawing on the screen.
    Write down what changes you see as you increase N by 1, starting at $N=3$ and finishing at $N=10$.
2. Look at the equation $A = 360/N$.
    Write down the value of A for each value of N from 3 to 10.
    By increasing N, what happens to the external angle A?
    Does this agree with any comment you have made in task 1?
3. The angle on a straight line is 180°.
    Write down the internal angle of POLY, given that the external angle is A.
    Write down the value of $180-A$ for each value of A in task 2.
    By increasing N, what happens to the internal angle $180-A$?
    Does this agree with any comment you have made in task 1?
4. Draw on triangle paper or by using a template a regular hexagon and mark on the paper where you think the angles A ($=360/N$) and $180-A$ ($=180-360/N$) are.
    Repeat for a square.
5. Experiment with the POLY procedure and use it to draw what looks like a circle.
6. The type of Logo you are using will determine the effective size of SIDE. The following calls of POLY :SIDE :N using Logotron Logo all produce what appear to be the same sized circles. Why?

        POLY 40 30
        POLY 30 40
        POLY 20 60
        POLY 10 120

    If you cannot answer this yet, try to work through the following questions and tasks:
    (a) How much has the turtle turned from beginning to end for each of the POLY calls?
    (b) How many *times* has it turned after completing POLY 40 30?
    (c) Complete the following table:

	:SIDE	:N	360/:N (=A)	A/:SIDE
POLY	40	30		
POLY	30	40		
POLY	20	60		
POLY	10	120		

(d) Can you describe what you think the numbers in the last column have to do with the size of the circles?

(e) Complete the following table and compare the results in the last column with those in task (c):

	:SIDE	:N	360/:N (=A)	A/:SIDE
POLY	20	30		
POLY	15	40		
POLY	10	60		
POLY	5	120		

Can you suggest more calls of POLY which will have the same effect?

The last column measures how much *turn per unit step* (curvature) the turtle makes, so it is not surprising that these numbers are all the same for each table.

(f) Work out from each table the product :SIDE * :N.

Again the figure is the same for each table, and is a measure of how far the turtle has travelled: in effect the circumference C of each circle. For the second table $C = 600$; the equation connecting circumference with radius is $C = 2\pi r$, so $r = 300/\pi$ which is approximately 95.493.

(g) Recalculate the final column (curvature) in the second table, but this time use 2π radians instead of 360 degrees. What is the connection between this value and 95.493?

7. Now that we know something about how regular polygons are drawn and how they relate to circles, consider how to change the POLY procedure in order to draw part of a circle, i.e. an arc, and call this procedure POLYARC. (Some versions of Logo have an arc drawing procedure built into the set of primitives.) Note that the version of POLYARC given in the appendix to this chapter does not always give an arc of D degrees when D is input. For example, the procedure as written in Logotron Logo with an input :SIDE=30 :N=25 :D=60° gives a turn of 57.6°: can you say why? For an arc drawing procedure which gives an accurate amount of turn every time, we have to REPEAT D times and turn through 1°. So for a given radius we have to move by an amount equal to 2π x radius/360:

```
TO ARC :RADIUS :D
REPEAT :D [FD :RADIUS * 2 * 3.14159 / 360 RT 1]
END
```

8. Use ARC to draw petals of various sizes (Figure 7.4).
    If pupils find it difficult to decide what to do at point B, consider how far the turtle has been turned by ARC in moving from A to B. We can of course use the input angle D in order to reason what action should be taken at B, but it can also be illustrated by drawing tangents to the curve at A and B.

Figure 7.4 **Petal formation**

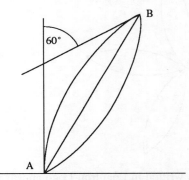

Let us assume that the turtle starts with its heading at zero and turns through 60° as it moves along the arc from A to B. Its heading at B will be 60°. In order to make a petal which has (bilateral) symmetry we need to change the turtle's heading to 180° before the second arc is drawn. We can do this by turning RIGHT (180 − 60) degrees. Figure 7.5 illustrates the angles involved for arcs which turn through 60°. So in moving from A to B and back to A we have a total turtle trip of 60 + 120 + 60 + 120 = 360°, or more generally $D + (180 - D) + D + (180 - D) = 360°$

Figure 7.5 **Angles turned in petal formation**

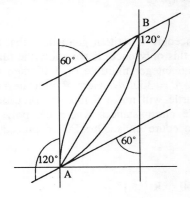

Can you argue this through if the turtle heading was not zero to begin with?

9. Use PETAL as a subprocedure to FLOWER to draw various types of flowers (Figure 7.6).

Figure 7.6 **FLOWER 300 60 5**

Some answers written in Logotron Logo appear in the appendix to this chapter.

More advanced uses of Logo

It is possible to move in other directions to develop further aspects of geometry and number work by using the POLY procedure as a starting point:

```
TO POLY :SIDE :N
REPEAT :N [FD :SIDE RT 360 / :N]
END
```

The way in which the POLY procedure is written guarantees that the turtle turns a full 360°, and does this only once. If we allow the turtle to turn more than this, say by an integer multiple of 360° then the equation $A = 360/N$ changes to $A = 360R/N$. Here R indicates the number of complete turns the turtle will make before the procedure stops. As we will see, there are circumstances where the polygon appears complete before the procedure ends. Our POLY procedure now becomes:

```
TO NEWPOLY :SIDE :N :R
REPEAT :N [FD :SIDE RT 360 * :R / :N]
END
```

Figure 7.7 **NEWPOLY 200 5 1**

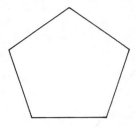

Figure 7.8 **NEWPOLY 200 5 2**

Procedure calls NEWPOLY 200 5 1 and NEWPOLY 200 5 2 produce Figures 7.7 and 7.8 respectively. It seems reasonable to ask if there could be any more variants to the familiar regular pentagon. There are two fairly obvious ways forward at this point. One is to try the other procedure calls NEWPOLY 200 5 3 and NEWPOLY 200 5 4, see what happens and then decide why such shapes appear; the other is to look at the mathematics at work in the procedure in order to predict what will happen. The results of the last two calls are shown as part of the output from the FAMILY procedure (see later), but the mathematics is not difficult. We need to look at the expression $360R/N$ for N fixed at 5 and for R at 1 through to 4:

R	1	2	3	4
$360R/5$	72	144	216	288

These are the external angles through which the turtle turns RIGHT. So a right turn of 216° is the same as a left turn of $360-216 = 144°$, and a right turn of 288° is the same as a left turn of 72°. This suggests that angles used by NEWPOLY which lie between 180° and 360° produce mirror images of those polygons produced by their conjugate angles. The procedure FAMILY draws all the figures for a given value of N:

```
TO FAMILY :N
MAKE "C 1
REPEAT :N - 1 [NEWPOLY 200 :N :C MAKE "C :C + 1]
END
```

Figure 7.9 **FAMILY 5**

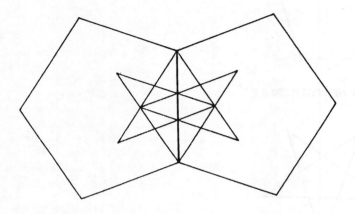

Figure 7.10 **FAMILY 8**

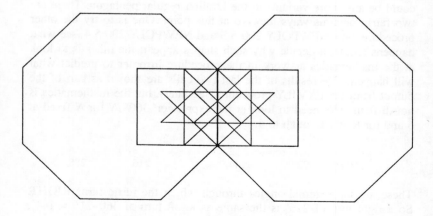

The results of procedure calls FAMILY 5 and FAMILY 8 are shown in Figures 7.9 and 7.10 respectively. You will notice that FAMILY 8 appears to have only six members and that only two of these (ignoring mirror images) have eight sides. Why should this be so? Again a look at the expression $360R/N$ for each value of R tells us where the 'hidden' shape is and why there are two squares in the family:

R	1	2	3	4	5	6	7
$360R/8$	45	90	135	180	225	270	315

Squares are produced when R is 2 or when R is 6, and a straight line is produced when R is 4.

It now becomes evident that the relationship between R and N is quite crucial in determining the kind of shape produced by NEWPOLY. If R and N have a common factor then the fraction R/N can be reduced to its lowest terms. In a similar way the figure produced by NEWPOLY is reduced to a simpler form. I find the simplistic nature of this connection between fraction and figure rather appealing. Readers might like to conjecture what a call of FAMILY :N, where N is prime, will produce and check it using their own version of Logo.

Before leaving NEWPOLY let us consider a slightly more powerful version which draws other 'families' of new polygons:

```
TO NEWPOLYF :SIDE :N :R :F
REPEAT :N [NEWPOLY :SIDE :N :R + :F FD :SIDE RT 360 * :R / :N]
END
```

NEWPOLYF draws a polygon or star polygon whose shape is determined by R. A procedure call NEWPOLYF 250 5 1 1 produces the shape in Figure 7.11, and other members of the five-sided family which are linked in this way are equally accessible. NEWPOLYF has eight distinct members and eight mirror images. For example, NEWPOLYF 250 5 1 2 and its mirror image NEWPOLYF 250 5 4 3 produce the shape in Figure 7.12. Can you determine other pairs by looking at the parameters to NEWPOLYF?

NEWPOLYF 250 5 1 1 holds many golden ratios ($\phi = (1 + \sqrt{5})/2$: see Gardner 1961:69). For instance there are three different sizes of the regular pentagram (five-pointed star) within Figure 7.11. If AC is taken to be a side length of the middle-sized star, how are their side lengths related? Let us assume that the smallest stars have a side length of 1; then the largest star has a side length of 2. It remains for us to determine the side length of the middle-sized star in relation to these two lengths, i.e. the ratios 2:AC and AC:1. The ratio equivalence AC/1 = 1/CL holds using corresponding lengths of the stars, and since CL = AC–1 we have AC/1 = 1/(AC–1). So $AC^2 - AC - 1 = 0$, and

Figure 7.11 **NEWPOLYF 250 5 1 1**

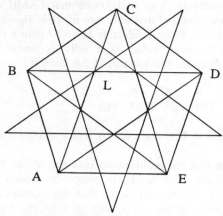

Figure 7.12 **NEWPOLYF 250 5 1 2; NEWPOLYF 250 5 4 3**

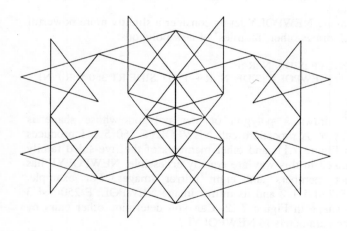

hence AC = $(1 + \sqrt{5})/2$ or $(1 - \sqrt{5})/2$. Taking the positive sign gives the ratio of the side lengths of the middle-sized star to the side lengths of the small star. So we have AC:1 = ϕ and 2:AC = 2:ϕ.

It is hoped that some of this discussion has encouraged readers to use turtle graphics as another resource through which to pose and solve problems in mathematics. It is not possible here to cover the many uses of Logo, and those of you already familiar with Logo will be aware that only a very small part of the language has been covered. Advanced Logo ideas are to be found in Abelson and diSessa (1981). There is just one aspect of the language that must feature in any coverage of the implications for learning mathematics through Logo programming; this is the notion of recursion. In relatively simple procedures like the polygon procedures, recursion can be used in a way which has a similar effect to repeating a set of instructions. This is achieved by making the last instruction in a procedure a procedure call to the same procedure. This type of recursion is often called *tail recursion* and is relatively easy to understand. For example the polygon drawing procedure POLY can be written recursively since the means to a 'solution' lies in repeating a piece of code over and over again. The recursive version of POLY follows:

```
TO POLY :SIDE :N
FD :SIDE RT 360 / :N
POLY :SIDE :N
END
```

Note that this version has no means of stopping, so drawing will continue after the polygon is complete. Our previous experience tells us that if we want to stop the procedure when the polygon is first complete then we have to take account of the total turn achieved by the turtle, and that this will be an integer multiple of 360°. As an exercise, the reader might like to write such a procedure (hint: use another parameter to store the total turn and use the REMAINDER function available on most versions of Logo).

There are other uses of tail recursion, some not connected with turtle graphics, and some where tail recursion is not the only recursion employed. These are generally more difficult to understand. I will give just a few examples.

Consider the function which simply doubles any value in its domain, and take the set of positive integers (including zero) to be this domain. The familiar way of describing such a function would be $f(x) = 2x$ $(x \in Z^+)$. However, it can be defined inductively by evaluating f for a few elements in its domain and then giving a recurrence relation in order to calculate all other values of f from the previous few. An inductive definition follows:

$$f(0) = 0$$
$$f(n) = f(n\text{-}1) + 2 \text{ for } n \geq 0$$

Olson (1987:151) talks about the use of Logo in order to 'reconceptualize' a static problem as a dynamic one. This example shows precisely how this can be achieved. The inductive definition can now be coded recursively as follows:

```
TO TIMES2 :N
IF 0 = :N [OP 0 STOP]
OP ( TIMES2 :N – 1 ) + 2
END
```

This essentially turns the problem from one involving multiplication to one of repeated addition, and so for large values of *N* the procedure will be relatively slow to compute the final value. A generalization of this procedure to calculate the product of any two numbers is only a small step away:

```
TO TIMES :N :M
IF 0 = :N [OP 0 STOP]
OP ( TIMES :N – 1 :M ) + :M
END
```

Similarly the factorial function FAC :N (=*N*!, where *N* is a positive integer), which is often given in Logo programming books as a first example of a recursive procedure, easily follows from the examples above:

```
TO FAC :N
IF 0 = :N [OP 1 STOP]
OP ( :N * FAC :N – 1 )
END
```

In the discussion about the 'village streets' problem in Chapter 6 you will recall that the addition of the *n*th street to the previous *n*–1 streets in the village added another n–1 intersections, provided it did not pass through any previous intersection. A procedure which is recursively defined appears to be a more natural way of solving this problem. The recurrence relation is

posts(1) = 0
posts(streets) = posts(streets–1) + streets–1 (streets≥1)

This is easily coded to become:

```
TO POSTS :STREETS
IF 1 = :STREETS [OP 0 STOP]
OP ( POSTS :STREETS – 1 ) + :STREETS – 1
END
```

Recursion which has a less obvious outcome occurs either when a procedure call to itself is not the last statement of the procedure, or when more than one such call is made. The following examples are less easy to follow but they nevertheless have a similar pattern to their structure. The first is the familiar tree drawing procedure (see Figure 7.13):

Figure 7.13 **TREE 200**

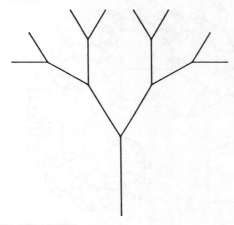

```
TO TREE :BRANCH
IF 70> :BRANCH [STOP]
FD :BRANCH RT 30
TREE ( :BRANCH * 3 / 4 )
LT 60
TREE ( :BRANCH * 3 / 4 )
RT 30
BK :BRANCH
END
```

This procedure, in common with all the previous ones, can be made more general in order to produce trees with branches at different angles, and branches whose length in relation to the lengths of previous branches is different from 3/4. However, the main difference lies in where the procedure calls itself. The first call of TREE actually draws the right-hand branches and the second call of TREE produces the left-hand branches. Further tree variations are possible by adding subprocedures which draw shapes instead of straight lines for branches. The procedure EXPTREE uses Pythagoras' theorem to connect squares with triangles which in turn form the branches of the tree. Many variations are possible simply by changing parameters. For example, calls of EXPTREE 100 30 0.5 1 and EXPTREE 100 160 0.5 1 produce Figures 7.14 and 7.15. A listing of EXPTREE can be found in the appendix to this chapter, and a fuller discussion of this particular procedure can be found in Simmons (1987).

Figure 7.14 **EXPTREE 100 30 0.5 1**

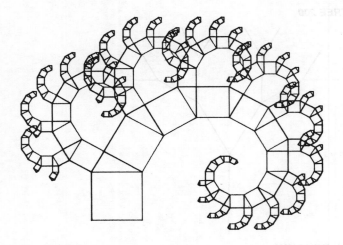

Figure 7.15 **EXPTREE 100 160 0.5 1**

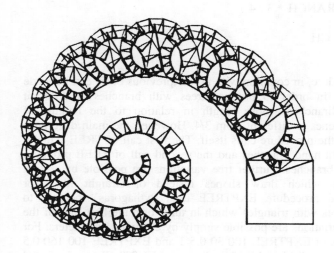

A problem which has a solution structure similar to the tree drawing procedure is the towers of Hanoi problem. This particular problem is well documented and is used increasingly as a class problem-solving exercise. The problem (Figure 7.16) is to move a given number of discs from peg 1 to peg 3 via peg 2. The rules are that only one disc may be moved at a time and that no disc must be placed on top of a smaller disc. Pupils determine the most efficient algorithm, make a table of results for various numbers of discs and attempt to generalize their results. Before reading on you should familiarize yourself with the problem and attempt to do the same.

Figure 7.16 **Towers of Hanoi with three disks**

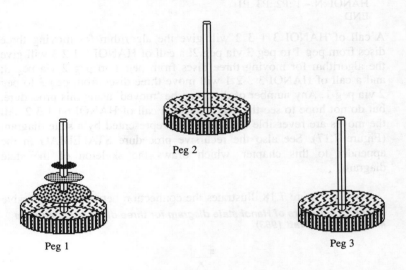

Peg 2

Peg 1

Peg 3

The results for *n* discs are:

No. of discs	1	2	3	4	5	6	. . .
Minimum no. of moves	1	3	7	15	31	63	. . .

Here again the generalization $f(n) = 2^n - 1$, where *n* is a positive integer, represents the 'function' approach, but it does not represent the way in which the problem is solved. Those who have experimented with this problem will realize that it naturally divides itself into three stages:

1. Move *n*–1 discs from peg 1 to peg 2.
2. Move the *n*th disc from peg 1 to peg 3.
3. Move *n*–1 discs from peg 2 to peg 3.

So if we can complete the first stage in *N* ways we can also complete the third stage in N ways; hence we can move n discs in $2N+1$ ways. This forms the basis of the recurrence relation which connects the number of moves for n-1 discs with the number of moves for n discs. Readers may also like to try a proof by induction. This together with the three macro moves forms the basis for the following recursive procedure, again written in Logotron Logo:

```
TO HANOI :N :P1 :P3 :P2
IF 0 = :N [STOP]
HANOI :N – 1 :P1 :P2 :P3
TYPE [MOVE DISC] TYPE :N TYPE [FROM PEG] TYPE :P1 TYPE
[TO PEG]
PRINT :P3
HANOI :N – 1 :P2 :P3 :P1
END
```

A call of HANOI 3 1 3 2 will give the algorithm for moving three discs from peg 1 to peg 3 via peg 2; a call of HANOI 3 1 2 3 will give the algorithm for moving three discs from peg 1 to peg 2 via peg 3; and a call of HANOI 3 3 2 1 will move three discs from peg 3 to peg 2 via peg 1. Any number of discs can be 'moved' using this procedure, but do not hope to see the end result to a call of HANOI 64 1 3 2. All the moves are reversible and all can be represented by a state diagram (Figure 7.17). See also the recursive procedure STATEDIAG in the appendix to this chapter, which draws the skeleton of the state diagram.

Finally, Figure 7.18 illustrates the connection between the recursive

Figure 7.17 **Towers of Hanoi state diagram for three discs (adapted from McGregor and Watt 1983)**

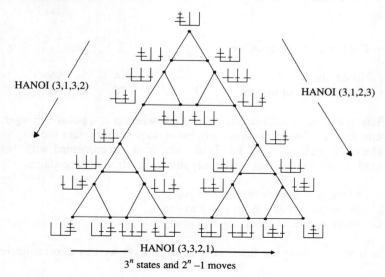

HANOI (3,1,3,2)

HANOI (3,1,2,3)

HANOI (3,3,2,1)

3^n states and $2^n - 1$ moves

procedure TREE and the recursive procedure HANOI. The tree, which is trunkless, is on its side and the recursive calls of HANOI are inserted at the branch points. The initial call is HANOI 3 1 3 2. Note that the print statements which indicate how a disc is to be moved occur when a move is made from a top branch to a bottom branch in the tree structure. The circled numerals indicate the order in which the procedure operates, and the lower-case roman numerals indicate the order in which the information is output.

Figure 7.18 **Procedure resulting from HANOI 3 1 3 2. Numerals ①to⑭ indicate procedure order. Printing occurs when a move is made from a top to a bottom branch (i.e. from ③ to ④ etc.): symbols (i) to (vii) indicate order of printing**

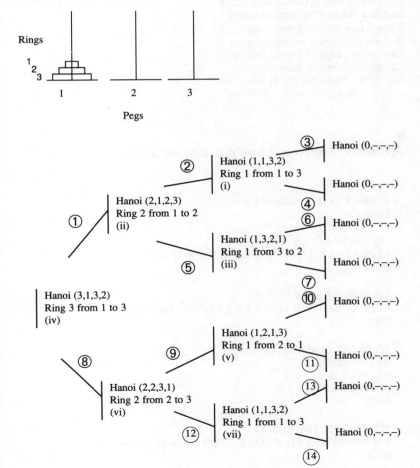

Concluding remarks

The various chapters of this book have sought to bring, to those embarking upon a teaching career in mathematics, themes which the author considers important in establishing necessary skills and attitudes. It is hoped that the glimpses into the research behind the various theories will encourage teachers not only to pursue their own interests from a theoretical perspective but to consider the implications of such research for future practice. We owe it to future generations to develop our teaching expertise alongside the newer technologies through a process of learning, implementation and reflection. Enjoy your teaching!

We've trod the maze of error round,
Long wandering in the winding glade;
And now the torch of truth is found,
It only show us where we strayed;
By long experience taught, we know,
Can rightly judge of friends and foes;
Can all the worth of these allow,
And all the faults discern in those.
                    George Crabbe (1754–1832)

Appendix: Logotron Logo procedures used

```
TO POLY :SIDE :N
REPEAT :N [FD :SIDE RT 360 / :N]
END

TO POLYARC :SIDE :N :D
REPEAT :N * :D / 360 [FD :SIDE RT 360 / :N]
END

TO ARC :RADIUS :D
REPEAT :D [FD :RADIUS * 2 * 3.14159 / 360 RT 1]
END

TO PETAL :RADIUS :D
ARC :RADIUS :D
RT 180 – :D
ARC :RADIUS :D
END

TO FLOWER :RADIUS :D :P
REPEAT :P [PETAL :RADIUS :D RT 180 – :D RT 360 / :P]
END
```

```
TO NEWPOLY :SIDE :N :R
REPEAT :N [FD :SIDE RT 360 * :R / :N]
END

TO FAMILY :N
MAKE "C 1
REPEAT :N – 1 [NEWPOLY 200 :N :C MAKE "C :C + 1]
END

TO NEWPOLYF :SIDE :N :R :F
REPEAT :N [NEWPOLY :SIDE :N :R + :F FD :SIDE RT 360 * :R / :N]
END

TO RPOLY :SIDE :N
FD :SIDE RT 360 / :N
RPOLY :SIDE :N
END

TO TIMES2 :N
IF 0 = :N [OP 0 STOP]
OP ( TIMES2 :N – 1 ) + 2
END

TO TIMES :N :M
IF 0 = :N [OP 0 STOP]
OP ( TIMES :N – 1 :M ) + :M
END

TO FAC :N
IF 0 = :N [OP 1 STOP]
OP ( :N * FAC :N –1 )
END

TO POSTS :STREETS
IF 1 = :STREETS [OP 0 STOP]
OP ( POSTS :STREETS – 1 ) + :STREETS – 1
END

TO TREE :BRANCH
IF 70>  :BRANCH [STOP]
FD :BRANCH RT 30
TREE ( :BRANCH * 3 / 4 )
LT 60
TREE ( :BRANCH * 3 / 4 )
RT 30
BK :BRANCH
END
```

```
TO HANOI :N :P1 :P3 :P2
IF 0 = :N [STOP]
HANOI :N – 1 :P1 :P2 :P3
TYPE [MOVE DISC] TYPE :N TYPE [FROM PEG] TYPE :P1 TYPE
[TO PEG] PRINT :P3
HANOI :N – 1 :P2 :P3 :P1
END

TO STATEDIAG :SIDE
IF 90> :SIDE [STOP]
REPEAT 3 [STATEDIAG :SIDE / 2 FD :SIDE RT 120]
END
```

BIBLIOGRAPHY

Abelson H., di Sessa A. 1981 *Turtle Geometry: the Computer as a Medium for Exploring Mathematics* MIT Press

Ahmed A. 1985 *Mathematics for Low Attainers: Some Classroom Activities and Approaches.* West Sussex Institute of Higher Education

Ahmed A. 1987 *Better Mathematics: a Curriculum Development Study* HMSO

Arcavi A., Bruckheimer M. 1981 How shall we teach the multiplication of negative numbers? *Mathematics in School* November: 31–3

Austin J.L., Howson A.G. 1979 Language and mathematical education *Educational Studies in Mathematics* 10(2): 161–97

Barnes D. 1976 *From Communication to Curriculum* Penguin

Beeney R. 1979 Mirror fun *Mathematics Teaching*: 33 Association of Teachers of Mathematics

Bell A.W., Rook D., Wigley A.R. 1975 *Journey into Mathematics* South Notts Project, Shell Centre for Mathematical Education, University of Nottingham

Bell A., Fletcher T. 1964 *Symmetry Groups* Association of Teachers of Mathematics

Bennett N., Desforges C. 1985 *Recent Advances in Classroom Research* Scottish Academic Press (*British Journal of Educational Psychology* monograph series no. 2)

Bloom B.S. 1956 *Taxonomy of Educational Objectives: the Classification of Educational Goals* Longman

Brissenden T.H.F. 1988 *Talking about Mathematics* Basil Blackwell

Buchanan N.K. 1987 Factors in problem solving performance *Educational Studies in Mathematics* 18(4): 399–415

Burton L. 1984 *Thinking Things Through: Problem Solving in Mathematics* Basil Blackwell

Cadwell J.H. 1966 *Topics in Recreational Mathematics* Cambridge University Press

Caldwell A.P.K. 1970 'I thought you were going to tell us about automorphisms' In Association of Teachers of Mathematics *Mathematical Reflections* Cambridge University Press

Carpenter T.P., Fennema E., Peterson P.L., Carey D.A. 1988 Teachers' pedagogical content knowledge of students' problem solving in elementary arithmetic *Journal for Research in Mathematics Education* 19(5): 385–401

Clark R.E. 1983 Reconsidering research on learning from media *Review of Educational Research.* 53(4): 445–59

Clements D.H., Gullo D.F. 1984 Effects of computer programming on young children's cognition *Journal of Educational Psychology* 76(6): 1051–8

Coolidge J.L. 1990 *The Mathematics of Great Amateurs* 2nd edn, Oxford University Press

Cope P., Simmons M. 1991 Children's exploration of rotation and angle in limited Logo microworlds *Computers and Education.* 16(2): 133–41

Cope P., Smith H., Simmons M. 1992 Misconceptions concerning rotation and angle in Logo *Journal of Computer Assisted Learning* 8: 16–24

Coxeter H.S.M. 1961 *Introduction to Geometry* Wiley

Coxeter H.S.M., Emmer M., Penrose R., Teuber M.L 1986 *M.C. Escher: Art and Science* Elsevier

Crowe D.W. 1981 The Geometry of African Art. In Davis C., Grunbaum B., Sherk F.A. (eds) *The Geometric Vein: the Coxeter Festschrift* Springer

Davis C., Grunbaum B., Sherk F.A. (eds) 1981 *The Geometric Vein: the Coxeter Festschrift* Springer

de Corte E., Verschaffel L. 1986 Effects of computer experience on children's thinking skills *Journal of Structural Learning* 9: 161–7

de Corte E., Verschaffel L. 1989 Logo: a vehicle for thinking. In Greer B., Mulhern G. (eds) *New Directions in Mathematics Education* Routledge, Chapter 3

DES 1982 *Mathematics Counts: Report of the Committee of Inquiry into the Teaching of Mathematics in Schools* (the Cockcroft Report) HMSO

DES 1985 *Mathematics from 5 to 16: Curriculum Matters 3* (HMI series) HMSO

DES 1988 *Mathematics for Ages 5 to 16* DES/WO

DES 1989 *Mathematics in the National Curriculum* HMSO

Desforges C., Cockburn A. 1987 *Understanding the Mathematics Teacher: a Study of Practice in First Schools* Falmer Press

Dessart D.J., Suydam M.N. 1983 In Dessart D.J. (ed) *Classroom Ideas from Research on Secondary School Mathematics* National Council of Teachers of Mathematics, Reston, Virginia

Dolan D.T., Williamson J. 1983 *Teaching Problem-Solving Strategies* Addison-Wesley

Ernest P. (ed.) 1987 *Teaching and Learning Mathematics Parts 1 and 2* School of Education, University of Exeter

Fenn A. 1930 *Abstract Design* Batsford
Fletcher T.J. 1983 *Microcomputers and Mathematics in Schools* DES
Freudenthal H. 1973 *Mathematics as an Educational Task.* Reidel
Gardiner A. 1987 (a) *Discovering Mathematics.* Oxford University Press
Gardiner A. 1987 (b) *Mathematical Puzzling* Oxford University Press
Gardner M. 1961 *More Mathematical Puzzles and Diversions* Pelican
Gattegno, C. 1963 *For the Teaching of Mathematics* vol. 1, Educational Explorers
Goddijn A. 1980 *Shadow and Depth* IOWO, Utrecht
Green O. 1985 Cognitive theory and Curriculum Design: A discussion of Thompson's Paper. In Silver E.A. (ed.) *Teaching and Learning Mathematical Problem Solving* Lawrence Erlbaum
Grouws D.A. 1988 One point of view *Arithmetic Teacher* 36(2): 6
Hart K., Johnson D.C., Brown M., Dickson L., Clarkson R. 1989 *Children's Mathematical Frameworks 8–13: a Study of Classroom Teaching* NFER/Nelson
Hembree R., Dessart D.J. 1986 Effects of hand-held calculators in precollege mathematics education: a meta-analysis *Journal for Research in Mathematics Education* 17(2): 83–99
Hiebert J., Wearne D. Procedures Over Concepts: The Acquisition of Decimal Number Knowledge. In Hiebert J. (ed.) 1986 *Conceptual and Procedural Knowledge: the Case of Mathematics* Lawrence Erlbaum
Hiebert J. 1988 A theory of developing competence with written mathematics symbols *Educational Studies in Mathematics* 19(3): 333–55
Higgo J., Hobbs D., Milner W., Perkins M., Tall D., Watson J., Wynne Wilson W. 1985 *132 Short Programs for the Mathematics Classroom* Mathematical Association
Holding J. 1991 *The investigations book* Cambridge University Press
House P.A. 1980 Risking the journey into problem solving. In NCTM *Problem Solving in School Mathematics.* National Council of Teachers of Mathematics, Reston, Virginia
Hoyles C. 1985 What is the point of group discussion in mathematics? *Educational Studies in Mathematics* 16(2): 205–14
Hoyles C., Sutherland R. 1989 *Logo Mathematics in the Classroom* Routledge
Kerslake D. 1986 *Fractions: Children's Strategies and Errors* NFER/Nelson
Kilpatrick J. 1985 A retrospective account of the past 25 years of research on teaching mathematical problem solving. In Silver E.A. (ed.) *Teaching and Learning Mathematical Problem Solving* Lawrence Erlbaum, 1–15 Kent Mathematics Project (KMP) Ward Lock Educational

Krasnor L.R., Mitterer J.O. 1984 Logo and the development of general problem-solving skills *The Alberta Journal of Educational Research* XXX(2): 133–44

Krathwohl D.R., Bloom B.S., Masia B.B. 1964 *Taxonomy of Educational Objectives: the Classification of Goals: Affective Domain* McKay

Kulik J.A., Bangert R.L., Williams G.W. 1983 Effects of computer-based teaching on secondary school students *Journal of Educational Psychology* 75(1): 19–26

Leinhardt G., Smith D.A. 1985 Expertise in mathematics instruction: subject matter knowledge *Journal of Educational Psychology* 77(3): 247–71

MacGillavry C.H. 1965 *Symmetry Aspects of M.C. Escher's Periodic Drawings* A Oosthoek's Uitgeversmaatschappij, Utrecht

Mack N.K. 1990 Learning fractions with understanding: building on informal knowledge *Journal for Research in Mathematics Education* 21(1): 16–32

Mason J. 1985 *Thinking Mathematically* Addison-Wesley

Mason J., Pimm D. 1986 *Discussion in the Mathematics Classroom PM644 Open University*

Mathematics in Action Group *Mathematics in Action* Blackie-Chambers

Maurer 1987 New Knowledge about Errors and New Views about Learners: What they Mean to Educators and More Educators would like to know. In Schoenfeld A.H. (ed.) *Cognitive Science and Mathematics Education* Lawrence Erlbaum

McGregor J., Watt A. 1983 *Advanced Programming Techniques for the BBC Micro* Addison-Wesley

Noss R., Hoyles C. 1987 Structuring the mathematical environment: the dialectic of process and content. In Hillel J. (ed.) *Proceedings of Third International Conference for Logo and Mathematics Education* Concordia University, Montreal

Olson A.T. 1987 The curricular implications of recursion. In Hillel J. (ed.) *Proceedings of Third International Conference for Logo and Mathematics Education* Concordia University, Montreal

Orton A. 1987 *Learning Mathematics: Issues. Theory and Classroom Practice* Cassell

Papert S. 1980 *Mindstorms: Children, Computers and Powerful Ideas* Harvester

Parker A., Straker N. 1989 Kepler's method *Mathematics in School* 18(4): 38–9

Pea R.D. 1987 Cognitive Technologies for Mathematics Education. In Schoenfeld A.H. (ed.) *Cognitive Science and Mathematics Education* Lawrence Erlbaum

Phillips R. 1980 *Grasses, Ferns, Mosses and Lichens of Great Britain and Ireland* Pan

Piaget J. 1928 *Judgement and Reasoning in the Child* London: Kegan Paul Ltd

Pimm D. 1987 *Speaking Mathematically: Communication in Mathematics Classrooms* Routledge and Kegan Paul

Pirie S.E.B. 1988 Understanding: instrumental, relational, intuitive, constructed, formalised . . .? How can we know? *For the Learning of Mathematics* 8(3): 2–6

Pirie S.E.B., Schwarzenberger R.L.E. 1988 Mathematical discussion and mathematical understanding *Educational Studies in Mathematics* 19(4): 459–70

Polya G. 1945 *How to Solve It: a New Aspect of Mathematical Method* Princeton University Press

Raphael D., Wahlstrom M. 1989 The influence of instructional aids on mathematics achievement *Journal for Research in Mathematics Education* 20(2): 173–90

Renzulli J.S. 1977 *The Enrichment Triad Model: a Guide for Developing Defensible Programs for the Gifted and Talented* Creative Learning Press

Rosen J. 1975 *Symmetry Discovered* Cambridge University Press

Schoenfeld A.H. 1979 Can Heuristics be taught? *Cognitive Process Instruction* Franklin Institute Press

Schoenfeld A.H. 1980 Heuristics in the Classroom. In NCTM *Problem Solving in School Mathematics* National Council of Teachers of Mathematics, Reston, Virginia

SEC 1986 *Mathematics GCSE: a Guide for Teachers* Secondary Examinations Council with the Open University

SED 1990 *Mathematics 5–14: Curriculum and Assessment in Scotland: a Policy for the 90s* Report of the Review and Development Group on Mathematics for Scotland, working paper no. 3

Shulman L.S. 1985 On teaching problem solving and solving the problems of teaching. In Silver E.A. (ed.) *Teaching and Learning Mathematical Problem Solving* Lawrence Erlbaum

Shulman L.S. 1986 Those who understand: knowledge growth in teaching *Educational Researcher* 15: 4–14

Silver E.A. 1986 Using Conceptual and Procedural Knowledge: A Focus on Relationships. In Hiebert J. (ed.) *Conceptual and Procedural Knowledge: the Case of Mathematics.* Lawrence Erlbaum

Silver E.A. 1985 Research on Teaching Mathematical Problem Solving: Some Underrepresented Themes and Needed Directions. In Silver E.A. (ed.) *Teaching and Learning Mathematical Problem Solving* Lawrence Erlbaum

Simmons M. 1987 Maths with Logo *Educational Computing* 8(6): 49–51

Simmons M. 1990 Possibility spaces *Micromath* 6(2): 19–21

Simmons M., Cope P. 1990 Fragile knowledge of angle in turtle geometry *Educational Studies in Mathematics* 21: 375–82

Skemp R.R. 1971 *The Psychology of Learning Mathematics* Penguin

Skemp R.R. 1985 *Primary Mathematics Project for the Intelligent Teaching of Mathematics: a Progress Report* University of Warwick

Slavin R.E. 1980 Cooperative learning *Review of Educational Research* 50(2): 315–42

SMP 11–16 *School Mathematics Project* Cambridge University Press

SMILE Mathematics Smile Centre London

Steen L.A. 1986 Living with a New Mathematical Species. In Howson A.G. Kahane J.P. *The Influence of Computers and Informatics on Mathematics and its Teaching* Cambridge University Press

Sutherland R. 1989 Providing a computer based framework for algebraic thinking *Educational Studies in Mathematics* 20(3): 317–44

Suydam M.N. 1982 The use of Calculators in Pre-college Education: Fifth Annual State-of-the-art Review Eric Document ED 220–273

Suydam M.N. 1980 Untangling clues from Research on Problem Solving. In NCTM *Problem Solving in School Mathematics* National Council of Teachers of Mathematics, Reston, Virginia

Swing S.R., Peterson P.L. 1982 The relationship of student ability and small-group interaction to student achievement *American Educational Research Journal* 19(2): 259–74

Travers K.J., Pikaart L., Suydam M.N., Runion G.E. 1977 *Mathematics Teaching* Harper and Row

van Hiele P.M. 1986 *Structure and Insight: a Theory of Mathematics Education* Academic Press

Walter M. *Readings in Mathematical Education: Geometry* Association of Teachers of Mathematics

Webb N.M. 1982 Student interaction and learning in small groups *Review of Educational Research* 52 (3): 421–45

Webb N.M 1983 Predicting learning from student interaction: defining the interaction variables *Educational Psychologist* 18(1): 33–41

Wells D. 1988 *Hidden Connections, Double Meanings* Cambridge University Press

Weyl H. 1952 *Symmetry* Princeton University Press

Wickelgren W.A. 1974 *How to Solve Problems: Elements of a Theory of Problems and Problem Solving* W.H. Freeman

Williams F.E. 1970 *Classroom Ideas for Encouraging Thinking and Feeling* DOK Buffalo

Index